Ready Notes

to accompany

Foundations of Physical Education and Sport

Fourteenth Edition

Deborah A. Wuest
Ithaca College

Charles A. Bucher

Boston   Burr Ridge, IL   Dubuque, IA   Madison, WI   New York   San Francisco   St. Louis
Bangkok   Bogotá   Caracas   Kuala Lumpur   Lisbon   London   Madrid   Mexico City
Milan   Montreal   New Delhi   Santiago   Seoul   Singapore   Sydney   Taipei   Toronto

The McGraw-Hill Companies

Ready Notes to accompany
FOUNDATIONS OF PHYSICAL EDUCATION AND SPORT
Deborah A. Wuest, Charles A. Bucher

Published by McGraw-Hill, an imprint of The McGraw-Hill Companies, Inc., 1221 Avenue of the Americas, New York, NY 10020. Copyright © 2003 (1999) by The McGraw-Hill Companies, Inc.

1 2 3 4 5 6 7 8 9 0 QPD/QPD 0 9 8 7 6 5 4 3 2

ISBN 0-07-246228-0

Chapter 1: Nature and Scope of Physical Education, Exercise Science, and Sport

- What is "contemporary physical education?"
- How do different areas of physical education relate to the field overall?
- What is the importance of creating your personal philosophy of physical education, exercise science, and sport?

 Goals for Physical Educators

- Access to physical education and sport for all, regardless of: age, gender, race, ethnicity, sexual orientation, disability status, income, educational level, geographic location and ability.
- Prevent disease and positively contribute to health and well-being of all participants.

Expansion of Physical Education, Exercise Science, and Sport

- Moved from the traditional school setting to:
  - Community
  - Home
  - Worksite
  - Commercial & Medical Settings
  - Corporations

Who says Physical Activity is Good?

- National Reports:
  - "Physical Activity and Health: A Report of the Surgeon General"
  - "Healthy People 2010"
  - "Promoting Better Health for Young People through Physical Activity and Sports"

Physical Activity and Health A REPORT OF THE SURGEON GENERAL

HEALTHY PEOPLE 2010

Our Physical Activity Challenge:
Improve Participation of Populations with Low Rates of Physical Activity

Current Participation Patterns:

- Women are generally less active than men at all ages.
- African Americans and Hispanics are generally less active than whites.
- People with low incomes are typically not as active as those with high incomes.
- People with less education are generally not as active as those with higher levels of education.
- Adults in the Northeast and South tend to be less active than adults in the North Central and Western States
- People with disabilities are less physically active than people without disabilities.
- Participation in physical activity declines with age. By age 75, one in 3 men and one in two women engage in no physical activity.

U.S. Department of Health and Human Services. Healthy People 2010: Understanding and Improving Health. Washington, DC: U.S. Government Printing Office, November, 2000.

Definitions: Physical Education

- Physical education....
  - An educational process that uses physical activity as a means to help people acquire skills, fitness, knowledge, and attitudes that contribute to their optimal development and well-being.
  - Contributes to the development of the whole person.
- Education
  - An on-going process that occurs throughout our lifespan.

Definitions: Exercise Science

- Exercise Science...
  - The scientific analysis of exercise or physical activity through theories from many different disciplines such as biology, biochemistry, physics, and psychology.

Definitions: Sports

- Organized competitive activities governed by rules that standardize the competition and conditions so individuals can compete fairly.
- Competition against oneself or opponent(s).
- Strategy and skill play a significant role in the determination of the outcome.

Definition: Athletics

- Highly organized, competitive sports
- Skillful participants

The Field (More than a playing surface!)

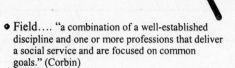

- Field…. "a combination of a well-established discipline and one or more professions that deliver a social service and are focused on common goals." (Corbin)

- Discipline …"organized body of knowledge embraced in a formal course of learning." (Henry)

Physical Education, Exercise Science and Sport: The Profession

- Profession…
  - An occupation requiring specialized training in an intellectual field of study that is dedicated to the betterment of society through service to others.
- Some examples of professional organizations:

NATIONAL ASSOCIATION FOR SPORT & PHYSICAL EDUCATION

AAHPERD
American Alliance for
Health Physical Education
Recreation and Dance

Organizing The Profession

- With developing technologies, knowledge, and methods of inquiry from other disciplines in the 1960s, physical education, exercise science, and sport broadened its horizons to incorporate the fields of **psychology** and **sociology**.
- The result: 12 subdisciplines

Subdisciplines

- Exercise physiology
- Sports medicine
- Sport biomechanics
- Sport philosophy
- Sport history
- Sport psychology

- Motor development
- Motor learning
- Sport sociology
- Sport pedagogy
- Adapted physical activity
- Sport management

 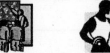

Exercise Physiology (Chapter 7)

- Impact of exercise and physical activity on the human body.
- Short- and long-term adaptations of the various systems of the body.
- Effects of physical activity and exercise on the health status of different populations.
- ACSM: *AMERICAN COLLEGE of SPORTS MEDICINE*

Sports Medicine (Chapter 12)

- Medical relationship between physical activity, sports-related injuries, and the human body.
- Prevention - the design of conditioning programs, fitting of protective equipment, and counseling regarding proper nutrition.
- Treatment and rehabilitation - the assessment of injuries, administration of first aid, design and implementation of rehabilitation program and treatment.

National Athletic Trainers' Association

Sport Biomechanics (Chapter 6)

- Applies the methods of physics to the study of human motion and the motion of sport objects.
- Study the effects of force on the body and sport objects.
- Mechanical analysis of activities (production of power, leverage, and stability)
- Analysis of effectiveness and efficiency of movements

_____

_____

_____

_____

_____

_____

_____

Sport Philosophy (Chapter 1)

- Study of the nature of reality and values of movement for all participants.

- Debate critical issues, beliefs, and values relative to physical education and sport (i.e. What is the relationship between the mind and the body?).

- Influences thoughts, actions, and decisions in our professional endeavors and personal lives.

_____

_____

_____

_____

_____

_____

Sport History (Chapter 5)

- Critical examination of the past with a focus on events, people, and trends that influenced the direction of the field.
- The "who, what, when, where, how, and why of sport" is examined within the social context of the time.
- Looking into the past provides greater understanding of present events and insight with respect to the future.

NASSH: North American Society for Sport History publishes the Journal of Sport History.

_____

_____

_____

_____

_____

_____

Sport and Exercise Psychology (Chapter 9)

- Uses principles from psychology to study human behavior in sport to enhance performance.
- <u>Sport areas</u>: achievement motivation, arousal regulation, goal setting, self-confidence, leadership, and team cohesion
- <u>Exercise areas</u>: exercise addiction, adherence, motivation, and satisfaction

---

Sport and Exercise Psychology (Chapter 9)

◆Uses principles from psychology to study human behavior in sport to enhance performance.

- <u>Sport areas</u>:
  - achievement motivation
  - arousal regulation
  - goal setting
  - self-confidence
  - leadership
  - team cohesion
- <u>Exercise areas</u>:
  - exercise addiction
  - adherence to exercise
  - motivation
  - satisfaction

Motor Development (Chapter 9)

- Interaction of genetic and environmental influences on movement and lifespan motor development.
- Use theories of development to design appropriate movement experiences for people of all ages and abilities.

Motor Learning (Chapter 9)

- Study of factors that influence an individual's acquisition and performance of skills, such as practice, experience, use of reinforcement, and condition of learning environment.
- Progression through stages of learning from a beginner to a highly skilled performer.

Sport Sociology (Chapter 8)

- Study of the role of sport in society.
- "What is the influence of society on sport?"
- "What is the influence of sport on society?"

Center for the Study of Sport in Society at Northeastern University publishes the Journal of Sport and Social Issues.

Sport Pedagogy (Chapter 11)

- Study of teaching and learning.
- Creation of effective learning environments, instructional strategies, outcome assessment, and relationship of instructional process to learning.
- Development of effective practitioners through the analysis of the behaviors of teachers/coaches and students/athletes.

Adapted Physical Activity (Chapter 11)

- Providing individual programs and services that encourage participation to the fullest extent by those with disabilities.

Sport Management (Chapter 13)

- Encompasses the managerial aspects of sport and sport enterprise.
- Facility and personnel management, budgeting, promotion of events, media relations, and programming.

The Journal of Sport Management is the official journal of the North American Society for Sport Management (NASSM).

A New Name for the Field

- Physical Education- traditional, but too narrow; does not reflect the expanding nature of the field.
- Kinesiology- study of human movement, but the public is not familiar with the term.
- Exercise and Sport Science- reflects the broad emphasis of the field and easy to understand.
- Physical Education and Sport- traditional, familiar, and includes sport as a vital part.
- No common agreement as to the name of the field, but there is a growing central focus: **Physical Activity**.

Allied Fields

- Health:
  - Health Instruction
  - Health Services
  - Environmental Health
- Recreation
- Dance

These fields share many purposes with physical education, exercise science, and sport, but the content of the subject matter and methods to reach their goals are different.

Definition of Terms

- Health: a state of positive well-being associated with freedom from disease or illness.
- Wellness: a state of positive biological and psychological well-being that encompasses a sense of well-being and quality of life.

Definition of Terms

- Holistic Health: the physical, mental, emotional, spiritual, social, environmental, and genetic factors' influence on an individual's life. (similar to wellness)
- Quality of Life: overall sense of well-being that has a different meaning for each individual.

Definition of Terms

- **Physical activity**: any bodily movement produced by the contraction of the skeletal muscles that increases energy expenditure above the baseline level.
- **Exercise**: physical activity that is planned, structured, and repetitive with the purpose of developing, improving, or maintaining physical fitness.

Definition of Terms

- **Physical Fitness**: the ability to perform daily tasks with vigor and without undue fatigue, and with sufficient energy to engage in leisure-time pursuits, to meet unforeseen emergencies, and the vitality to perform at one's fullest capacity.
- **Health-related** and **Performance-related** physical fitness: what are the components of each?

Physical Fitness

- **Health-related Fitness**
  - Cardiovascular endurance
  - Body composition
  - Flexibility
  - Muscular endurance
  - Muscular strength

- **Performance-related Fitness**
  - Agility
  - Speed
  - Coordination
  - Power
  - Reaction time
  - Balance

Philosophy

- "The love of wisdom" (Greek)
- A set of beliefs relating to a particular field.
- A system of values by which one lives and works.
- Helps individuals address the problems that confront them through the use of critical thinking, logical analysis, and reflective appraisal.

Branches of Philosophy

- <u>Metaphysics</u>- the ultimate nature of reality; what is real and exists.
- <u>Epistemology</u>- the nature of knowledge
- <u>Logic</u>- Examines ideas in an orderly manner and systematic way.
- <u>Axiology</u>- the nature of values
  - <u>Ethics</u>: issues of right and wrong, responsibility, and standards of conduct.
  - <u>Aesthetics</u>: the nature of beauty and art.

General Philosophies

- **Idealism**: The mind interprets events and creates reality; truth and values are absolute and universally shared.
- **Realism**: The physical world is the real world and it is governed by nature; science reveals the truth.
- **Pragmatism**: Reality and truth is determined by an individual's life experiences.
- **Naturalism**: Reality and life are governed by the laws of nature; the individual is more important than the society.
- **Existentialism**: Reality is based on human existence; individual experiences determine what is true.
- **Humanism**: Development of the full potential of each individual. Emphasized meeting the needs individuals' needs.

Philosophical Approaches

- "Education of the Physical"
  - Focus on fitness development and acquisition of skills; the development of the body.
- "Education through the Physical"
  - Focus on the development of the total person: Social, Emotional, Intellectual, and Physical development.

Sport Philosophy

- Study of the true meanings and actions of sport and how sport contributes to our lives.
  - Eclectic philosophy of education (1875-1950)
  - Comparative Systems Approach (1950-1965)
  - Disciplinary Approach (1965-present)
- Sport philosophy offers us guidance in addressing inequities in physical activity opportunities experienced by underserved populations.

Why develop your own philosophy?

- Assists in the development and clarification of beliefs and values that guide your behaviors.
- Aids in decision-making.
- Helps determine goals, objectives, and methods of instruction and evaluation used in physical education programs

Chapter 2: Objectives for Education and the Field of Physical Education and Sport

- What are the goals and objectives of physical education, exercise science, and sport in society?
- What is a physically educated person?
- Describe the three domains of behavior that affect development.
- Why is assessment important in physical education, exercise science, and sport?

Role of Education in Society

- Responsible for meeting the challenge of preparing today's students to live and work in an era of technological advances and great diversity.
- Active role in developing well-rounded, productive, self-directed citizens for the future.

What are Goals?

- General statements of purposes, intents, and aims that reflect desired long-term outcomes.

- Goal of contemporary physical education:
  - To help all people acquire the necessary knowledge, skills, and appreciations to participate in physical activity throughout their lifespan.

What are Objectives?

- Short-term statements of <u>specific</u> outcomes that build cumulatively to reach a goal.
- Describe the behavior that an individual will exhibit when the desired outcomes are achieved.

<u>**Four Components of Objectives:**</u>

- Goal component
- Performance or behavioral activity
- Criterion standard
- Condition

Goals 2000: Educate America Act

- <u>1994</u>: President Clinton signed these goals into law. Since then, these have become how we measure the progress of American education.
  - Readiness to learn
  - Improvement of graduation rates
  - Competency in core subjects
  - World leadership in math and science
  - Adult literacy
  - Positive and safe learning environment
  - Professional development of teachers
  - Parental involvement

Call to Action for American Education in the 21st Century (1997)

- Ten goals set for forth by President Clinton by this project included:
  - Development of rigorous national standards
  - Talented and dedicated teachers
  - Expansion of preschool programs and greater parental involvement
  - Increased use of technology
  - A learning environment that is safe, drug-free, disciplined, and instills American values
  - Increased educational accountability
  - Opening the doors of college to those who qualify

No Child Left Behind (2001)

- *Condition of Education 2000* revealed that there was an achievement gap between races and classes.
- In 2001, President G.W. Bush proposed *No Child Left Behind* to narrow this achievement gap.
  - Calls for the use of standards, assessment, accountability, flexibility, and parental choice to improve the quality of education for all.

Contributions of Quality Physical Education to the Goals of Education

- Development of the total person through motor skills and fitness.
- Enhances the health and well-being of students; promoting good health through the lifespan.
- Learning readiness through movement experiences.
- Integrated, multi-disciplinary educational curriculum

Individual Physical Educator's Contributions to Education

- "Physical education should contribute to the complete education of the individual."
  - Thomas Wood (1893)
- "Hygienic, educative, recreative, and remedial objectives…"
  - Dudley Sargent (1880s)
- "Organic, psychomotor, intellectual, and character education…"
  - Clark Hetherington (1910; Father of Modern Physical Education)
- "Physical (organic), motor and movement, mental, and social development…"
  - Charles Bucher (1964)

AAHPERD's Physical Education Goals and Objectives

- 1934: Physical fitness, mental health and efficiency, social-moral character, emotional expression and control, and appreciation.
- 1950: Develop and maintain maximum physical efficiency, acquire useful skills, to conduct oneself in socially useful ways, and to enjoy wholesome recreation.

AAHPERD's Physical Education Goals and Objectives

- 1965: "This is Physical Education"
  - Move in a skillful and effective manner.
  - Understanding and appreciation of movement.
  - Understanding and appreciation of scientific principles concerned with movement.
  - Improvement of interpersonal relationships.
  - Develop various organ systems of the body so they will respond in a healthful way to the increased demands placed upon them.

AAHPERD's Physical Education Goals and Objectives

- 1971: PEPI identifies a "physically educated" person as possessing knowledge and skill concerning his or her body and how it functions. Among the values highlighted:
  - PE is health insurance.
  - PE contributes to academic achievement.
  - PE provides skills and experiences that last a lifetime.
  - PE develops a positive self-image and ability to compete and cooperate with others.

NASPE's "A Physically Educated Person"... (1986)

NATIONAL ASSOCIATION
FOR SPORT & PHYSICAL
EDUCATION

- **HAS** learned the skills necessary to perform in a variety of physical activities
- **IS** physically fit
- **DOES** participate regularly in physical activity
- **KNOWS** the implications of and the benefits from involvement in physical activities
- **VALUES** physical activity and its contribution to a healthful lifestyle

(As a result of the NASPE Outcomes Project)

NASPE's Content Standards in Physical Education (1995)

- Standard 1: Demonstrates competency in many movement forms and proficiency in a few movement forms.
- Standard 2: Applies movement concepts and principles to learning of motor skills.
- Standard 3:Exhibits a physically active lifestyle.
- Standard 4: Achieves and maintains a health-enhancing level of physical fitness.

NASPE's Content Standards in Physical Education (1995) continued...

- Standard 5: Demonstrates responsible personal and social behavior.
- Standard 6: Demonstrates understanding and respect for differences among people.
- Standard 7:Understands that physical activity provides opportunities for enjoyment, challenge, self-expression, and social interaction.

(From *Moving Into the Future: National Standards for Physical Education*)

Learning Domains

- **Cognitive**
  - Acquisition and application of knowledge
- **Affective**
  - Values, social skills, and emotional development
- **Psychomotor**
  - Motor skills
  - Fitness

Cognitive Domain

- Development of intellectual skills.
- The acquisition of knowledge about the human body.
- Understanding of the relationships between the human body and physical activity and health.
- Application of movement concepts to learning and development of motor skills.
- Knowledge of technique, rules, strategies, and safety involved in physical activity.

Objectives for the Cognitive Domain

- Listed from lowest to highest levels of intelligence:
  - **Knowledge**: Memory; ability to recall information.
  - **Comprehension**: Understand material w/o perceiving implications.
  - **Application**:Can apply rules, methods and concepts.
  - **Analysis**: Ability to breakdown information into its parts.
  - **Synthesis**: Rebuilds pieces of information to form a new whole.
  - **Evaluation**: Judges values of ideas and concepts based on objective criteria or standards.

Affective Domain

The development of:
- Values
- Ethics
- Appreciations
- Attitudes
- Character development
- Cooperation
- Self-responsibility
- Self-concept and self-esteem
- Decision-making skills
- Self-management and control

Objectives of the Affective Domain

- **Receiving**: Awareness of stimuli.
- **Responding**: Attending to stimuli.
- **Valuing**: Can place worth and appreciation on stimuli.
- **Organizing**: Internalization and organization of values into a hierarchy.
- **Characterizing by a value or complex**: Individual's behaviors are consistent with internalized values; Part of personality.

Psychomotor Domain

- Motor skill development
  - Presented in a sequential manner from fundamental movements to complex, specialized sports skills
- Physical fitness development
- Development of the psychomotor domain is physical education's <u>unique</u> contribution to the education of children and youth!

Objectives of Psychomotor Domain

- Reflex movements
- Basic fundamental movements
- Perceptual abilities
- Physical abilities
- Skilled movements
- Communication through nonverbal expressions

Assessment of Learning

- NASPE identifies "the primary goal of assessment as the **enhancement of learning**, rather than the documentation of learning."
- <u>Assessment</u>: the use of a variety of techniques to gather information about the participants' achievement and make decisions based on the outcomes that will enhance the overall program.

Purposes of Assessment

- <u>Diagnosis</u>: Identify strengths and weaknesses of individuals.
- <u>Placement</u>: Ability grouping for instruction may facilitate learning.
- <u>Determination of achievement</u>: Have the participants achieved their objectives?
- <u>Motivation</u>: Encouraging participants to improve further.
- <u>Program evaluation</u>: Identify evidence of effectiveness or areas that need improvement.
- <u>Teacher effectiveness</u>: Appropriateness of instructional techniques for student learning.

Use of Assessment

- Assessment should be related to program goals and objectives.
- Assessment measures should be carefully selected.
  - Does it possess validity?
  - Does it possess reliability?
  - Does it possess objectivity?
  - Is it administratively feasible?

Types of Assessment

- <u>Formative</u>: Continual assessment of participants' progress throughout program.
- <u>Summative</u>: Assessment that occurs only at the end of the program.
- <u>Product</u>: Focuses on the end result of a performance; usually quantitative in nature.
- <u>Process</u>: Focuses on the quality of the performance; usually qualitative in nature.
- <u>Norm-referenced</u>: Comparing individual scores against established standards for a population group with similar characteristics.
- <u>Criterion-referenced</u>: Comparing individual scores against a predetermined standard of performance, not against other individuals.

Traditional Assessment

- Traditional assessment techniques
  - Multiple-choice tests
  - Psychosocial inventories
  - Standardized sport skills and fitness tests
- Dissatisfaction with traditional assessment
  - Too specific and narrowly focused
  - Too artificial: skills are assessed in isolation, instead of a natural setting.
  - Failure to measure important outcomes of interest to teachers and students.

Alternative Assessment

- Emphasizes *performance-based* outcomes requiring that participants demonstrate important competencies.
- May be perceived as more "informal" than traditional assessment methods, yet yield powerful information about participants' learning.
- Examples: Score sheets, checklists, running diary, self-reflections, peer evaluations

---

Authentic Assessment

- Assessment takes place in a **realistic situation** as opposed to an artificial setting often associated with traditional assessment.
- Modified game-like situations are used to assess the skills of the participants.
- Use of a scoring rubric or rating scale to guide the assessment process.

Role of Technology in Assessment

- Can be useful in record-keeping, regulation of testing equipment, and data analysis.
- Computer programs:
  - Cooper's Institute of Aerobics Fitnessgram
  - The Activitygram
  - Healthfirst TriFit system
- Heart-rate monitors
- Cybex
- Personal Digital Assistants (PDAs): Hand-held computers

Chapter 3: Role of Physical Education and Sport in Society and Education

◆ What are the implications of changing demographics in the U.S for physical education, exercise science, and sport?

◆ What is the fitness movement?

◆ What are the current educational reform movements is physical education, exercise science, and sport?

Changing Demographics

◆ Life expectancy is at an all time high:
  ↗ Public health initiatives
  ↗ Advances in medical science
  ↗ Improvements in standards of living

◆ Population is becoming older
  ↗ In 2000, 2% of population was 85 or older, by 2050, 5% of population will be 85 or older.
  ↗ By 2030, one in five will be over the age of 65.

Changing Demographics

◆ Society is becoming increasing diverse.
  ↗ 2000 Census: 75.2% white, 12.3% African American, 3.6% Asian, .9% American Indian/Alaskan Native, .1% Native Hawaiian, 2% multiracial.
  ↗ In 1999, 2.6 million school-age children spoke a language other than English at home, double that of 1979.

◆ Family structure is changing.
  ↗ 1970, married couple families with kids was 87%; in 2000, it was down to 69%.

◆ Poverty impacts on health and well-being.
  ↗ Almost 17% of children live below poverty line, affecting school outcomes and potential for future earnings.

Cultural Competence

- "...a set of congruent behaviors, attitudes, and policies that come together in a system, agency, or among professionals that enables effective work in cross-cultural situations."
  - **Culture**: integrated patterns of human behavior that include the language, thoughts, communications, actions, customs, values, and institutions of racial, ethnic, religious, or social groups.
  - **Competence**: having the capacity to function effectively as an individual and an organization within the context of cultural beliefs, behaviors, and needs presented by consumers and their communities.

Achieving Cultural Competence

- "...an on-going developmental process of personal reflection and growth."
  - Reflect on your own cultural heritage, beliefs and biases.
  - Understand how power, privilege, oppression, discrimination, and stereotypes influence opportunities for different cultural groups.
  - Gain knowledge of other cultures.
  - Show respect and compassion for cultural differences.

Achieving Cultural Competence

- Office of Minority Health produced guidelines for culturally competent health care: 14 standards for culturally and linguistically appropriate services (CLAS).
  - "...health organizations should ensure that patients receive from all staff members, effective, understandable, and respectful care that is provided in a manner compatible with their cultural beliefs, practices, and preferred language."
- U.S. Bureau of Primary Health Care:
  - "100% Access, 0 Disparities"

Wellness Movement

- ◆ Changes in the leading cause of death from infectious diseases to chronic diseases.
  - ↗ Chronic diseases account for 7 out of 10 deaths.
- ◆ Role of behavioral risk factors in disease and early mortality.
  - ↗ Cardiovascular disease is out nation's #1 cause of death, followed by cancer.
  - ↗ Estimated 60% of adults are overweight or obese.
  - ↗ Physical inactivity, poor diet, and being overweight contribute to at least 1/3 of all cancers.

Health defined...

- ◆ World Health Organization defines *health* as a "state of complete physical, mental, and social well-being and not merely the absence of disease and infirmity."
- ◆ Incorporates the physical, mental, and social aspects of health.

Wellness defined ...

- ◆ …state of optimal health and well-being.
- ◆ …living life to the fullest and maximizing one's potential as a whole person.
- ◆ … 5 components - physical, emotional, social, intellectual, and spiritual.
- ◆ …personal responsibility.
- ◆ …impact of heredity and social context.

National Health Reports

- ◆ Healthy People (1979)
  - ↗ Established national goals for improving health.
- ◆ Objectives for the Nation (1980)
  - ↗ 226 public health objectives to be reached by 1990.
- ◆ Healthy People 2000 (1990)
  - ↗ 3 goals to reach by 2000: increase healthy lifespan, reduce health disparities among populations groups, and access to health services for all.
- ◆ Healthy People 2010
  - ↗ Comprehensive emphasis on health promotion and disease prevention.

Healthy People 2010

- ◆ A blueprint for improving the health of individuals and the health status of the nation.
- ◆ <u>Two main goals</u> with 28 focus areas, and 467 specific objectives:
  - ↗ *Increase quality and years of healthy life*
  - ↗ *Eliminate health disparities* (differences that occur by gender, race and ethnicity, education and income, disability, geographic location, or sexual orientation)

Healthy People 2010

- ◆ 10 leading <u>health indicators</u> that have helped individuals, institutions, and communities plan actions to improve health and provide a way to measure progress…

  - •Physical Activity
  - •Overweight and Obesity
  - •Tobacco Use
  - •Substance Abuse
  - •Responsible Sexual Behavior

  - •Mental Health
  - •Injury and Violence
  - •Environmental Quality
  - •Immunization
  - •Access to Health Care

Importance of Physical Activity

- ◆ Regular physical activity:
  - ↗ helps maintain functional independence of elderly
  - ↗ prevents disease
  - ↗ assists in the management of many diseases
  - ↗ enhances the quality of life for **ALL**
  - ↗ reduces medical costs
  - ↗ increased productivity and decreased absenteeism at work and school
  - ↗ and many more…

Wellness Movement and Physical Education & Sport

- ◆ Receive skills, knowledge, and values for physically active lifestyle.
- ◆ School PE programs:
  - ↗ reach over 50 million children each year.
  - ↗ provide the foundation for participation in physical activity throughout one's lifespan.
- ◆ School worksite health promotion programs can reach over 5 million adults.
- ◆ Use of school as a community center

PE's Contribution to Healthy People 2010

- ◆ Provides a means to discuss how the use of tobacco, alcohol, and drug abuse are deterrents to fitness.
- ◆ Reinforce nutritional concepts and impact of nutrition on performance.
- ◆ Teaches stress reduction techniques or how physical activity can alleviate stress.
- ◆ Water safety instruction can help reduce the number of drownings, an objective of Healthy People 2010.

Task Force on Physical Activity (2001)

- ◆ Released a report identifying 6 interventions that were effective in increasing physical activity:
  - ↗ Point-of-decisions prompts
  - ↗ Community-wide campaigns
  - ↗ School-based physical education
  - ↗ Social Support Interventions in community settings
  - ↗ Individually adapted health behavior change
  - ↗ Increased access to physical activity (new facilities, walking trails, worksite programs, etc.)

1996: **Physical Activity and Health** A REPORT OF THE SURGEON GENERAL

- ◆ People of all ages can benefit from physical activity.
- ◆ People can improve their health by engaging in a moderate amount of physical activity on a regular basis.
- ◆ Greater health benefits can be achieved by increasing the amount of physical activity through changing the duration, frequency, or intensity of the effort.

Physical Activity and Health A REPORT OF THE SURGEON GENERAL

- ☑ Moderate physical activity is defined as physical activity that results in an energy expenditure of 150 calories a day or 1,000 a week.
- ☑ Moderate physical activity engaged in on most, if not, all days a week yields health benefits.
- ☑ Integration of moderate physical activity into one's lifestyle.

National Children and Youth Fitness Study I (1985) & II (1987)

- 1985: Two areas of concern:
  - Body composition and cardiorespiratory endurance
  - Only 36.3% of the students participated in daily school physical education.
- 1987: Two areas of concern:
  - Cardiorespiratory endurance and upper body strength
  - Only 36.4% of students had daily physical education.
- Overall, the nation's youth was fatter than those of 1960.

School Health Policies and Programs Study 2000

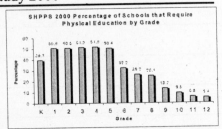

As stated in 1996 by the Surgeon General's report, this confirms that participation in physical activity declines as age or grade in school increases.

Centers for Disease Control amd Prevention 2000

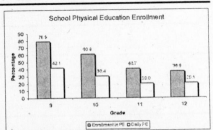

Again, as school grade levels increase, enrollment in physical education AND daily physical education decrease.

Youth Risk Behavior Surveillance System (YRBSS) 1990, 1991, 1993, 1995, 1997, & 1999

- ◆ Males were typically more active than females; they participated in more vigorous, moderate, and strengthening exercises than females.
- ◆ Caucasian students were more active than African Americans or Hispanic students.
- ◆ 57.2% of students reported that they watched television 2 hours or less during a school day.
- ◆ 56.1% were enrolled in physical education class, but only 29.1% participated in daily physical education.

National Health and Nutrition Examination Survey (NHANES)

- ◆ Designed to obtain information about the health and diet of children, youths, and adults.
- ◆ Uses the criteria of BMI value at or above the 95th percentile by age and sex to determine overweight.
- ◆ 1999: 13% of children 6-11, 14% of 12-19 year-olds were overweight.
- ◆ Prevalence of overweight adolescents increases the risk to become overweight adults, ultimately increasing the risk for many diseases.

Adults and Physical Activity and Health A REPORT OF THE SURGEON GENERAL

- ◆ About 15% of adults engage regularly in vigorous physical activity (3 times a week for 20 minutes).
- ◆ About 25% reported no physical activity during their leisure time.
- ◆ People with disabilities were more inactive than adults without disabilities.
- ◆ Physical activity is more prevalent among males than females; and Caucasians more than African Americans and Hispanics.
- ◆ Physical activity appears to decline with age.
- ◆ Walking is the most popular activity.

National Health Interview Survey (NHIS) 1997 and 1998

◆ 40% of adults (18 years and older) engaged in no leisure time activity.

◆ 18% of adults engaged in physical activities to improve and maintain muscular strength and endurance.

◆ 30% of adults performed stretching exercises.

◆ Time constraints, access to convenient facilities, unsafe environments, lack of motivation, and lack of knowledge are frequent reasons for the lack of physical activity.

Physical Activity and Adults

◆ Inactivity increases as age increased:
  ↗ 31% of 18-24 year-olds participated in no leisure time activity, compared to 65% of adults 75 and older.

◆ Inactivity decreased as the level of education attainment increased.

◆ Most popular activities for adults 18 and older:
  ↗ Walking (43.2%)
  ↗ Gardening or yard work (28.1%)
  ↗ Stretching exercises (27.2%)
  ↗ Weightlifting or strengthening exercises (15.5%)
  ↗ Biking or cycling (12.3%)
  ↗ Jogging or running (10.6%)

Physical Activity and Adults

◆ 61% of U.S. adults are either overweight or obese.

◆ 35% of adults were overweight, and 27% of adults were obese. This is and 8% increase from NHANES II (1976-1980).

◆ The picture of fitness and adults in our society is perplexing and contradictory---health club membership is booming, fitness participation remains steady, and overweight and obesity has reached epidemic proportions.

Physical Activity and Adults

- ◆ American Sports Data (ASD) tracks data for the health club industry and reported in 2000:
  - ↗ 20% of adults exercise frequently (more than 100 times each year).
  - ↗ Membership at health clubs increased nearly 50% during the 1990s, however, annual health club turnover rates remain between 30% and 40%.
  - ↗ Over 5 million people employ a personal trainer.
- ◆ Shift from cosmetic fitness to functional fitness

Physical Activity and Adults

- ◆ Sporting Goods Manufacturers Association reported in 2000:
  - ↗ Between 1990 and 2000, free-weight training by both sexes increased 67%.
  - ↗ Women outnumber men in fitness walking, treadmill exercise, and most other cardiovascular exercises.
  - ↗ Increases in purchasing of home exercise equipment and athletic footwear.
  - ↗ Community programs and facilities have increased.

CDC Recommendations

- ◆ Establish policies that promote enjoyable, lifelong physical activity.
- ◆ Provide safe, physical and social environments that encourage physical activity.
- ◆ Implement sequential physical education and health curriculums.
- ◆ Provide diverse extracurricular physical activity programs.
- ◆ Regularly evaluate physical activity instruction, programs, and facilities.

CDC Recommendations (cont.)

- Encourage parents and guardians to support their children's participation in physical activity and be physically active role models.
- Train teachers, coaches, staff, and community personnel to promote enjoyable, lifelong physical activity.
- Assess the physical activity patterns of young people.
- Provide a range of developmentally appropriate community sports and recreation programs to attract all young people.

Educational Reform 1970s & 1980s

- **Why?**
  - Public's desire for accountability
  - Poor reading and math performance by students
  - Reduction of academic standards for high school graduation
  - Relaxation of requirements for college entrance
  - Loss of professional status by teachers

Educational Reform

- **Improvement of student learning**
  - Greater emphasis on the basic subjects
  - Use of competency tests
  - More stringent graduation requirements
- **Improvement of teaching**
  - Continuing education for teachers
  - Competitive salaries
  - Career ladders and advancement
  - More stringent entrance requirements
  - Improvements in teacher preparation

Educational Reform (cont.)

- **Improvements in the organization of schools and their funding**
  - ↗ Lengthening of the school day and year
  - ↗ Formation of partnerships (schools and industries)
  - ↗ Increasing financial resources for economically disadvantaged school districts
- **Preparation of students to be lifelong learners**

The Condition of Education 1994

- All 50 states had implemented reforms.
- Almost all states had increased graduation requirements and mandated student-testing standards.
- More students are completing the recommended core curriculum.
- Math and science achievement increased.
- More students were attending college after graduating from high school.
- High school dropout rate decreased by nearly half.

The Goals 2000: Education America Act

- Established <u>goals</u> in 1994 for the year 2000 that would serve as benchmarks for progress in America's schools:
  - ↗ Emphasized a more challenging curriculum and higher academic standards.
  - ↗ U.S. students would be first in the world in math and science achievement.
  - ↗ Improvement of readiness of children entering school
  - ↗ Enhancing the professional development of teachers
  - ↗ Promoting great parental and community involvement.

The Condition of Education 2000 & 2001

- Improvements had been made in math and science, but still a long way to go.
- Reading and math achievement improved at all grade levels.
- Improved access to computers.
- More still needed to be done to enhance childhood readiness for school.

Disparities In Education

- Minorities are educationally disadvantaged.
- Those in poverty are more likely to have difficulty reading.
- Gender gap is slowly closing.
  - Females read and write better than males, although males perform better in math and science.
- Dropout rate differences across minorities.
  - Asian/Pacific Islander   3.8%
  - Caucasian, non-Hispanic   6.9%
  - African-American   13.1%
  - Hispanic   27.8%

Reasons for Educational Disadvantages

- Lower level of parental education
- Greater likelihood of living with a single parent
- Fewer community resources
- Disadvantaged schools less conducive to learning
- Greater likelihood of living in poverty
- Influx of English as a second language

Educational Reform and PE

- Is PE a "frill" and nonessential to curriculum?
  - There has been increased time in schools for core academic subjects, thus reducing time for physical education, music, and art.
- NASPE: PE should be an integral part of the school curriculum.
  - Physical education can affect both academic learning and the physical activity patterns of students.

_____

_____

_____

_____

_____

How does PE help educational achievement?

- Healthy children have more energy available for learning.
- PE is important for the overall education of students.
- Daily, quality PE programs can contribute to the attainment of our national health goals set out by _Healthy People 2010._
- Can reach disadvantaged children.
- Developing healthy habits at a young age can encourage lifelong healthy lifestyles.

_____

_____

_____

_____

_____

The 2001 _Shape of the Nation_

- Illinois is the only state requiring daily physical education for all students K-12.
- Many schools have waiver programs…
  - High physical competency test scores
  - Participation in community sports and community service activities
  - Medical reasons
  - Religious reasons
  - Participation in school sports, ROTC, marching band

_____

_____

_____

_____

_____

_____

The 2001 *Shape of the Nation*

- ◆ Time spent in physical education:
  - ↗ elementary level ranged from 30 to 150 minutes; NASPE recommends 150.
  - ↗ Middle school ranged from 80-275; NASPE recommends 275 minutes.
  - ↗ High school varied from 0-225; NASPE recommends 225.
- ◆ Most states have incorporated or are in the process of incorporating content standards for physical education.

Chapter 4: Movement: The Keystone of Physical Education and Sport

- ◆ Why is movement the cornerstone for physical education?
- ◆ What are examples for each of the four movement concepts?
- ◆ What are some suggestions to help individuals learn movement concepts and fundamental motor skills?

_____

_____

_____

_____

_____

_____

Concepts

- ◆ **Movement fundamentals**
  - ↗ Comprised of movement concepts and fundamental motor skills.
- ◆ **Movement concepts** are knowledge and understanding of movements that allow individuals to adapt and modify their movements to achieve specific movement goals. They include:
  - ↗ Body awareness
  - ↗ Spatial awareness
  - ↗ Qualities of movement
  - ↗ Relationships

_____

_____

_____

_____

_____

_____

Concepts

- ◆ **Fundamental motor skills** are the foundation for development of more complex and specialized motor skills used in games, sports, dance, and fitness activities.
- ◆ Ideally, movement concepts and fundamental motor skills should be learned during early childhood and <u>elementary</u> school.
- ◆ More likely to use these skills throughout lifetime when proficiency is achieved at a young age.

_____

_____

_____

_____

_____

_____

Two Approaches

- ◆ **Movement education**
  - ↗ Teachers present students with a series of problem-solving movement challenges to help students explore and understand their body.
  - ↗ Encourages individual creativity and the ability to adapt and modify movements.
- ◆ **Developmentally appropriate approach to physical education**
  - ↗ Meeting the developmental needs of the learner.
  - ↗ Develops competence, self-confidence in ability to move, and encourages regular participation in physical activity.

General Factors Affecting Movement

- ◆ **Physiological factors**
  - ↗ Cardiovascular endurance, muscular strength and endurance, and flexibility.
- ◆ **Psychological factors**
  - ↗ Fear, anxiety, self-confidence
- ◆ **Sociological factors**

  - ↗ Membership in a group can influence participation.
  - (ie. Families as good role models who are physically active.)
  - ↗ Gender roles
  - ↗ Economics

Movement Concepts

- ◆ <u>Body Awareness</u>: What can the body do?
- ◆ <u>Space Awareness</u>: Where does the body move?
- ◆ <u>Qualities of Movement</u>: How does the body move?
- ◆ <u>Relationships</u>: With whom and what does the body move?

Body Awareness Objectives

- Identification and location of body parts
- Body shapes and positions
- Awareness of body movements
- Body as a communicator to express feelings
- Awareness of muscle tension and relaxation

Spatial Awareness Objectives

- To recognize **self-space** and respect that of others
- To move within **general space** safely
- Recognize different **directions** and how to change directions
- To understand different **levels** of movement
- To travel through different **pathways** and the pathways that different objects move in.
- Adjusting **range** of movements according to the task and situation

Qualities of Movement Objectives

- **Balance**: Understand the nature of static and dynamic balance and the role of balance in movement.
- **Time**: Differentiate among speeds and to increase or decrease the speed of movement.
- **Force**: To be able to create and modify one's force to meet the demands of the task
- **Flow**:To combine movements smoothly and to perform movements within a restricted time or space.

Relationships Objectives

◆ To understand the relationship of body parts to one another and the body.

◆ To move effectively relative to other individuals and/or within a group.

◆ To understand the relationship between the body and its parts to objects.

Fundamental Motor Skills

◆ Three categories:
  ↗ Locomotor
  ↗ Nonlocomotor
  ↗ Manipulative

◆ Rate of progress in developing these skills varies with each individual.

◆ Several fundamental motor skills can be combined to create a specialized movement necessary in an activity.

◆ Lack of development may hinder future participation in activities.

Locomotor Movements

◆ Walking	◆ Leaping
◆ Running	◆ Skipping
◆ Jumping	◆ Sliding
◆ Hopping	◆ Galloping

Nonlocomotor Movements

- Bending and Stretching
- Twisting and Turning
- Pushing and Pulling
- Swinging

Manipulative Skills

- Throwing
- Catching
- Kicking
- Striking

Movement Education

- Rudolf Laban
- Progressive problem-solving by students
- Cognitive and creative involvement of students
- Explore, analyze, and apply knowledge to arrive at solutions; individual differences are appreciated.
- Teacher's role as a facilitator.

Developmental Approach

- "Developmentally Appropriate Physical Education Practices for Children" published by Council on Physical Education for Children (COPEC) in 1992.
- Educational experiences based on the cognitive, psychomotor, and affective needs of children
- Child-centered; Uniqueness of each child.
- Progressive sequencing
- Variety of teaching strategies
- Assessment

Teaching Suggestions

- Safe learning environment
- Child-centered instruction
- Practice opportunities
- Progression
- Accountability

Learning Across the Lifespan

- Instruction for adults takes place in a variety of settings.
- Rehabilitation and the re-teaching of skills.
- Practice and commitment by children and adults in order to change inefficient skills.
- Programs should be at appropriate developmental levels and provide a progressive sequence if learning experiences.

Chapter 5: Historical Foundations

- Trace the history of physical education, exercise science, and sport from earliest times to the present.
- Identify events that served as catalysts for physical education, exercise science, and sport's growth.
- What are recent developments in physical education, exercise science, and sport?

The Field of Sport History

- Emerged as a subdiscipline in the late 1960s and early 1970s.
- "... field of scholarly inquiry with multiple and often intersecting foci, including exercise, the body, play, games, athletics, sports, physical recreations, health, and leisure." (Struna)
- How has the past shaped sport and its experiences today?
- 1973: North American Society for Sport History held its first meeting.

Sample Areas of Study...

- How did urbanization influence the development of sports in America?
- How did the sports activities of Native Americans influence the recreational pursuits of the early colonists?
- How have Greek ideals influences the development of sportsmanship?

Ancient Nations: China

- ◆ Influence of isolation due to topography and Great Wall
- ◆ Influence of Taoism, Confucianism, and Buddhism which stressed the contemplative life
  - ↗ Physical activity meant individual freedom of expression, which was contrary to the ancient teachings.
- ◆ Con Fu gymnastics: To keep the body in good organic condition and ward off certain diseases caused by inactivity.
- ◆ <u>Activities</u>: wrestling, jujitsi, boxing, ts' u chu, ch'ui wan, shuttlecoach, and kite flying

Ancient Nations: India

- ◆ Strong religious influence of Buddism and Hinduism.
- ◆ Focus on spiritual needs, not the needs of the body and worldly things.
- ◆ Buddism emphasized right living and thinking, including self-denial, to help the soul reach a divine state.
- ◆ <u>Activities</u>
  - ↗ Yoga, throwing, tumbling, chariot races, riding elephants and horses, marbles, swordsmanship, dancing, wrestling, foot races

Ancient Nations: Ancient Near East

- ◆ Ancient Egypt, Assyria, Babylonia, Syria, Palestine, and Persia
  - ↗ believed in living a full life, including engaging in physical activity
- ◆ Influence from the military to build a stronger army
  - ↗ Emphasize strength, stamina, endurance, agility for imperialistic means, not for the individual.
- ◆ <u>Activities</u>
  - ↗ Gymnastics, horsemanship, bow and arrow, water activities, wrestling, jumping, hunting, fishing, physical conditioning for strength and stamina

Greece

- "Golden Age" of physical education and sport
- Striving for perfection, including physical development
- Vital part of the education of every Greek boy
  - ↗ "Exercise for the body and music for the soul"
  - ↗ Gymnastics - courage, discipline, and physical well-being, a sense of fair play, and **amateurism**
- National festivals

Greece - Sparta

- Main objective of physical education and sport was to build a powerful army.
- Individuals were subservient to the state and required to defend the state against enemies.
- Women and men were required to be in good physical condition.
- *agoge* - a system of public, compulsory physical training for young boys
- Activities
  - ↗ wrestling, jumping, running, javelin and discus, marching, horseback riding, and hunting

Greece: Athens (Sparta's antithesis)

- Democratic government
- Physical activity to develop bodies, for aesthetic value, and to live a more full, vigorous life.
- Gymnastics practiced in a *palaestra* and supervised by a *paidotribe*.
- Gymnasiums became the physical, social, and intellectual centers of Greece.
- Instruction was given by a *gymnast*.

Greece: National Festivals

- The **foundation** for the modern Olympic games.
  - ↗ Olympic Games first held in 776 B.C. and continued every 4 years until abolished by Romans in 394 A.D.
- Conducted in honor of a hero or deity
- Consisted of dancing, feasting, singing, and events of physical prowess
- Athletic events were the main attraction, although participation was mostly limited to **men**.
  - ↗ Rigid set of requirements for participation in the games, including amateurism
- **Truce** declared by all city-states during the time of the festivals
- Victors won a wreath of olive branches; highest **honor** that could be bestowed in Greece.

Rome

- Exercise for health and **military purposes**.
  - ↗ Rigid training schedule for soldiers: marching, running, jumping, swimming, throwing javelin and discus
- Greek gymnastics were introduced to Rome after the conquest of Greece but were not popular
  - ↗ Rome did not believe in the "body beautiful"
  - ↗ Preferred to be **spectators** rather than participants
  - ↗ Preferred **professionalism** to amateurism.
- Exciting "**blood sports**": gladiatorial combats and chariout races. "Duel to the death" or satisfaction of spectators.

Medieval Europe: The Dark Ages

- Fall of the Roman Empire (476 A.D.)
  - ↗ Physical and moral decay of the Roman people
- Physically strong Teutonic barbarians overran the Empire and brought the greatest **decline in learning** known to history.
- People participated in hunting, vigorous outdoor sport, and warfare, thus building strong, fit bodies.
- The spread of Christianity gave rise to **asceticism**.
- **Scholasticism**

Age of Feudalism (Between 9th and 14th centuries)

- ◆ Feudalism was a system of land tenure based on allegiance and service to the nobleman or the lord.
- ◆ Career opportunities for a nobleman's son:
  - ↗ Church - religious and academic education
  - ↗ Knighthood - education emphasized physical, social, and military training
- ◆ Knights

  - ↗ jousts and tournaments

Renaissance (14th to 16th centuries)

- ◆ Feudal system replaced by monarchies.
- ◆ Age of Enlightment, revival of learning, belief in dignity of human beings.
- ◆ Men were being educated with the invention of the printing press and establishment of more schools and universities.
- ◆ Humanism: "A sound mind in a sound body."

Renaissance

- ◆ Leaders
  - •Vittorino da Feltra
  - •Francois Rabelais
  - •Michel de Montaigne
  - •John Comenius
  - •John Milton
  - •Martin Luther
  - •John Locke
  - •John Jacques Rousseau
- ◆ Educational opportunities for the common people as well, but few for females.
- ◆ Class differences appear in participation of some sports.
- ◆ Physical education was important for learning, necessary for health, and preparation for warfare.

Modern Europe: Germany

- ◆ <u>Basedow</u> - inclusion of physical education in the school's curriculum.
- ◆ <u>Guts Muth</u> - "*Gymnastics for the Young*" and "*Games*" - illustrated various exercises and apparatus; explained the relationship of physical education to education
- ◆ <u>Jahn</u> - Turnverein societies to build strong and hardy citizens; *turnplatz* (exercise ground)

Modern Europe: Germany

- ◆ <u>Spiess</u> -Founder of school gymnastics in Germany.
  - ↗ Schools should be interested in the **total growth** of the individual; Physical education should receive the same consideration as other academic subjects
  - ↗ Adapted physical activity for girls and boys
  - ↗ Exercises combined with music
  - ↗ Progressive program

Modern Europe: Sweden

- ◆ Per Henik Ling
  - ↗ Scientific study of physical education
  - ↗ Establishment of training institutes
  - ↗ Design of gymnastic programs to meet specific individual needs
  - ↗ <u>3 Types</u>: Educational gymnastics, military gymnastics, and medical gymnastics
  - ↗ Teachers of physical education must have foundational knowledge of the effects of exercise on the human body.

Modern Europe: Sweden

- ◆ Branting
  - ↗ Devoted his time to medical gymnastics
  - ↗ Understanding of the effects of gymnastics on the muscular as well as nervous and circulatory systems
- ◆ Nyblaeus
  - ↗ Military gymnastics and the inclusion of women
- ◆ Hjalmar Fredick Ling
  - ↗ Organization of school gymnastics in Sweden for boys and girls.

Modern Europe: Denmark

- ◆ Nachtegall
  - ↗ Introduced physical education into the public schools
  - ↗ Teacher preparation
- ◆ Bukh
  - ↗ "primitive gymnastics" - build a perfect physique by performing exercises without cessation of movement.

Great Britain

- ◆ Home of outdoor sports
  - ↗ Wrestling, throwing, riding, fishing, hunting, swimming, rowing, skating, archery, hockey, quoits, tennis, football (soccer), cricket
- ◆ Maclaren -
  - ↗ Eager to make physical training a science; a system that was adopted by the British Army
  - ↗ Health is more important than strength
  - ↗ Exercise adapted to the individual
  - ↗ physical education essential in school curriculum

Influences of PE in the U.S.

- ◆ European ideals
  - ↗ Systems of gymnastics (exercises)
  - ↗ Philosophies of physical education
- ◆ Ancient Asian cultures
  - ↗ Yoga
  - ↗ Martial arts
  - ↗ Relationships between the mind, body, and spirit

Colonial Period (1607-1783)

- ◆ Colonists led an agrarian existence - physical activity through performing tasks essential to living and survival.
- ◆ Colonists brought sports with them from their native lands.
- ◆ Puritans denounced play as evil; recreational pursuits frowned upon.
- ◆ Reading, writing, and arithmetic in schools, not physical education.

National Period (1784-1861)

- ◆ Growth of private schools for females
- ◆ Introduction of German gymnastics to schools
- ◆ 1852: First intercollegiate competition: a crew race between Harvard and Yale.
- ◆ Catherine Beecher (1800-1878)
  - ↗ Calisthenics performed to music
  - ↗ One of the first to advocate for daily physical education
- ◆ Invention of baseball
- ◆ Horseracing, foot races, rowing, and gambling on sport events

Civil War Period until 1900

◆ Turnverein societies continue to grow and include both girls and boys
◆ **Dio Lewis**
  ↗ Programs for the "weak and feeble" in society
  ↗ Training school for teachers in Boston
  ↗ Inclusion of gymnastic programs in the schools
◆ **Nissen** - Swedish Movement Cure grows in popularity and recognized for its inherent medical values
◆ YMCA established; international training school at Springfield College

---

Civil War Period until 1900

◆ Growth of American sport in popularity
  ↗ Tennis
  ↗ Golf
  ↗ Bowling
  ↗ Basketball (Naismith)
◆ Founding of forerunner of Amateur Athletic Association (AAU)
◆ Revival of Olympics in Athens
◆ Colleges and universities develop departments and expand programs

---

Civil War Period until 1900

◆ Expansion of intercollegiate athletics
  ↗ Abuses raise concerns
  ↗ Establishment of governing bodies
◆ Emphasis on teacher preparation, scientific basis of PE, diagnosis and prescription of activity
◆ Organized PE programs in elementary and secondary schools
◆ 1885 - Founding of the forerunner of AAHPERD
◆ "Battle of the Systems" (Which system of gymnastics should be included in curriculum?)

Early Twentieth Century (1900s-1940s)

- Extensive interscholastic programs - controversy over programs for girls
- Growth of intramural programs and emphasis on games and sports in our programs
- Increased concern for the physically underdeveloped in our society
- Playground movement
- Higher standards for teacher training (4 year preparation)
- NCAA established to monitor collegiate athletics

World War I (1916-1919)

- Physical educators developed conditioning programs for armed forces .
- After the war, health statistics revealed that the nation was in poor shape (1/3 of men were physically unfit for armed service).
- Growth and upgrade of PE programs in schools following war due to legislation in some states.

Golden Twenties (1920-1929)

- Move away from formal systems of gymnastics toward games, sports, and valuable recreation and leisure time.
- "New" physical education emphasized contribution to the **total** development of the individual; "education through the physical" vs. "education of the physical".
- Calls for **reform of collegiate athletics** due to increasing professionalism, public entertainment, and commercialization.
- Women's programs increase staff, activities, required participation, and facilities.

Depression Years (1930-1939)

- ◆ Economic forces lead to cutbacks in PE programs and growth of recreational programs.
  - ↗ Between 1932 and 1934, nearly 40% of all physical education programs were dropped completely.
- ◆ Physical educators more involved in recreational programs for the unemployed.
- ◆ Growth of interscholastic, intercollegiate and women's programs.
- ◆ 1940: National Association of Intercollegiate Basketball became National Association of Intercollegiate Athletics in 1952

Mid-twentieth Century (1940-1970)

- ◆ Impact of WW II - physical training programs
- ◆ Physical fitness movement
  - ↗ President's Council on Physical Fitness and Sports
- ◆ Athletics
  - ↗ Increase opportunities for girls and women
  - ↗ Increased interest in lifetime sports
  - ↗ Sport programs below high school level increase
  - ↗ Increased number of intramural programs

Mid-twentieth Century (1940-1970)

- ◆ Professional preparation
  - ↗ Colleges and universities increase programs for teachers
  - ↗ American College of Sports Medicine (1954)
  - ↗ National Athletic Trainers' Association (1950)
- ◆ Programs for individuals with disabilities
  - ↗ Special Olympics (1968)
- ◆ Research grows in importance and becomes increasingly specialized

Significant Recent Developments

◆ Emergence of subdisciplines
◆ Disease prevention and health promotion
  ⬈ Healthy People
  ⬈ Objectives for the Nation
  ⬈ Healthy People 2000
  ⬈ Healthy People 2010
  ⬈ Surgeon General's Report on Physical Activity and Health
◆ Legislation promoting opportunities for girls and women, and people with disabilities
◆ Increased technology

School Physical Education

◆ Recognition of the critical role school PE in achieving national health goals
◆ Fitness status and physical activity of children and youth
◆ Congressional support for high-quality, daily physical education
◆ Daily PE declines from 42% to 25%

School Physical Education

◆ National Content Standards offer a national framework
◆ Emergence of new curricular models
◆ Only one state, Illinois, requires daily PE for all students, K-12

Physical Fitness and Participation in Physical Activity

◆ Expansion of the fitness movement and involvement in physical activity
◆ Shift from performance to health-related fitness to an emphasis on moderate-intensity physical activity
◆ Physical inactivity recognized as a major health problem

The Growth of Sport

◆ Phenomenal growth of participation in sports at all levels
◆ Youth sports involve more than 25 million children
◆ Interscholastic sports involve more than 6 million boys and girls
  ↗ Trend toward early specialization

The Growth of Sport

◆ Intercollegiate sports involve over 450,000 athletes
  ↗ Growth of sport as "big business" in some institutions
◆ Growth of recreational sport leagues and amateur sports for adults of all ages
◆ Professional sports continue to expand

Girls and Women in Sport

- Rapid growth since the passage of Title IX in 1972
- Changes in governance of intercollegiate sports
- Challenges to Title IX
- Changes in physical education classes following passage of Title IX

Programs for Individuals with Disabilities

- Federal Legislation
  - PL 93-122 Section 504 of the Rehabilitation Act
  - PL 94-142 Education of All Handicapped Children Act of 1975
  - Amateur Sports Act of 1978
  - PL 101-336 Americans with Disabilities Act
- Paralympics

Olympics

- Rebirth of the Olympics in 1896
- Centennial Olympics celebrated in Atlanta in 1996
- Politicization of the Olympic Games
- Evolving definitions of amateurism
- "Fairness" issues in the Olympics
- Addition of non-traditional sports
- Commercialization of the Olympics

Technology

- Computer technology and sophisticated research equipment
- Has led to record-breaking achievements for elite athletes in nearly all sports
- Facility improvement
- Fitness tests data available in schools with addition of heart rate monitors

U.S. Leaders in Physical Education

- Beck
- Follen
- Beecher
- Winship
- Dio Lewis
- Nissen
- Anderson
- Homans

- Hemenway
- Delsarte
- Sloane
- Roberts
- Durant
- Sargent
- Hitchcock

U.S. Leaders in Physical Education

- Posse
- McKenzie
- Bancroft
- Hanna
- McCurdy
- Gulick
- Riis

- Hetherington
- Nash
- Wood
- Cassidy
- Williams
- Brace
- Rogers

Chapter 6: Biomechanical Foundations of Physical Education and Sport

◆ What is the value of biomechanics for physical education, exercise science, and sport?

◆ Explain the meaning of mechanical principles and concepts that relate to motion, stability, leverage, and force. How are these used in sport techniques and physical skills?

Kinesiology

◆ Scientific study of human movement

◆ Anatomical and physiological elements that carry out movements

◆ Purposes of kinesiology
  ↗ Move safely
  ↗ Move effectively
  ↗ Move efficiently

Biomechanics

◆ The application of the principles of mechanical physics to understand movements and actions of human bodies and sport implements.

◆ Kinesiology and biomechanics are intricately related.

◆ Principles of these two fields can be applied to the fields of biology, physiology, engineering, physical and occupational therapy, and medicine as well.

Historical Development

- ◆ Biomechanics emerged from physical education as a specialized are of study in the mid-1960s and 1970s.
- ◆ Kinesiology Era (late 1800s- early 1900s)
  - ↗ Application of mechanics to the study of movement
  - ↗ Nils Posse: "The Special Kinesiology of Educational Gymnastics"
- ◆ Biomechanics Era (mid-20th century)
  - ↗ Increased teaching, research and writing
- ◆ Development of Biomechanics (1960s-present)
  - ↗ Differentiation between kinesiology and biomechanics, and application of biomechanics to physical education and sport.

Professional Development

- ◆ 1963: AAHPERD forms Kinesiology Section, and in 1993 became known as Biomechanics Academy
- ◆ 1973: International Society of Biomechanics
- ◆ 1976: American Society of Biomechanics
- ◆ 1982: International Society for Biomechanics in Sport (ISBS)
- ◆ Journals
  - ↗ 1968: *Journal of Biomechanics*
  - ↗ 1985: *Journal of Applied Biomechanics*
  - ↗ 2002: *Sports Biomechanics* (ISBS)

United States Olympic Committee

- ◆ Encouraged the development of biomechanics for the improvement of elite athletes' performances.
- ◆ Olympic Training Centers offer state-of-the-art care and technology for the testing and analysis of performance.

Reasons for Studying Biomechanics

- ◆ Better understanding of the human body and the various internal and external forces that affect movement.
- ◆ Offers scientific knowledge that can improve performance
- ◆ To improve sport techniques, equipment, and safety
- ◆ To design and conduct programs to enhance individual movement skills (Adapted PE)

Areas of Specialization

- ◆ **Developmental biomechanics**
  - ↗ Studies movement patterns and how they change across the lifespan and varying disabilities.
- ◆ **Biomechanics of exercise**
  - ↗ To maximize the benefits of exercise and reduce the chances of injury.
- ◆ **Rehabilitation mechanics**
  - ↗ Study of the movement patterns of people who are injured or who have a disability.
- ◆ **Equipment design**
  - ↗ Increases in performance through the change of equipment.

Major Areas of Study

- ◆ Biological aspects underlying human movement
- ◆ Mechanics
  - ↗ <u>Statics:</u> Study of factors relating to nonmoving systems or those characterized by steady motion.
  - ↗ <u>Dynamics:</u> Study of mechanical factors that relate to systems in motion
    - » Kinematics
    - » Kinetics

Sample Research Questions

- ◆ How do running motions change as children develop?
- ◆ How do forces summate to produce maximum power in the tennis serve
- ◆ How can athletic shoes be designed to reduce injuries on artificial turf?
- ◆ What is the best body position for swimming the butterfly stroke?

Biomechanical Terms

- ◆ Velocity
  - ↗ Speed and direction of the body
- ◆ Acceleration
  - ↗ Change in velocity involving the speed or direction
- ◆ Angular velocity
  - ↗ Angle that is rotated in a given unit of time
- ◆ Angular acceleration
  - ↗ Change of angular velocity for a unit of time

Biomechanical Terms

- ◆ Mass
  - ↗ Amount of matter possessed by an object
- ◆ Force
  - ↗ Any action that changes or tends to change the motion of an object
- ◆ Pressure
  - ↗ Ratio of force to the area over which force is applied

Biomechanical Terms

- ◆ Gravity
  - ↗ Natural force that pulls all objects toward the center of the earth
  - ↗ Center of gravity
- ◆ Friction
  - ↗ Force that occurs when surfaces come in contact and results from the sliding of one surface on the other

Biomechanical Terms

- ◆ Work
  - ↗ Force that is applied to a body through a distance and in direction of the force
- ◆ Power
  - ↗ Amount of work accomplished in one unit of time

Biomechanical Terms

- ◆ Energy
  - ↗ Capacity of the body to perform work
    - » Kinetic energy
    - » Potential energy
- ◆ Torque
  - ↗ Twisting, turning, or rotary force related to the production of angular acceleration

Mechanical Principle: Stability

◆ The lower the center of gravity to the base of support, the greater the stability.
◆ The nearer the center of gravity to the center of the base of support, the more stable the body.
◆ Stability can be increased by widening the base of support.

Mechanical Principle: Motion

◆ Newton's First Law
  ↗ Law of inertia
◆ Newton's Second Law
  ↗ Law of Acceleration
◆ Newton's Third Law
  ↗ Law of Action and Reaction

Motion

◆ Linear Motion
  ↗ Movement in a straight line and from one point to another.
◆ Rotary motion
  ↗ Movement of a body around a center of rotation called an axis.

Mechanical Principle: Leverage

- Lever - mechanical device used to produce a turning motion around a fixed point called an *axis*.
- Lever components
  - Fulcrum - center or axis of rotation
  - Force arm - distance from the fulcrum to the point of application of the force
  - Resistance arm - distance from the fulcrum to the weight on which the force is acting

Levers

- First class - fulcrum between the weight and the force
- Second class - weight is between the fulcrum and the force
- Third class - force is between the fulcrum and the weight

Mechanical Principle: Force

- The effect that one body has on another.
- Production of Force
  - Produced by the actions of muscles. The stronger the muscles, the more force the body can produce.
- Application of Force
  - The force of an object is most effective when it is applied in the direction that the object is to travel.
- Absorption of Force
  - The impact of a force should be gradually reduced ("give with the force") and spread over a large surface.

Instruments

- ◆ Computers
  - ↗ Simulation
- ◆ Cinematography
- ◆ Stroboscopy
- ◆ Videography

- ◆ Anthropometry
- ◆ Timing devices
- ◆ Electrogoniometry
- ◆ Electromyography
- ◆ Dynamography
- ◆ Telemetry

Analysis

- ◆ **Quantitative Analysis**
  - ↗ Produced through the use of instruments.

- ◆ **Qualitative Analysis** (observation suggestions)
  - ↗ Position yourself to see the critical components of the skill. Use multiple vantage points.
  - ↗ Observe performance several times to identify consistent performance problems.
  - ↗ Use the whole-part-whole observation method.
  - ↗ Be sure to focus both on the performer and the implement.
  - ↗ Evaluate the overall effectiveness of the movement.
  - ↗ Use a performance checklist to guide your efforts.

The Future

- ◆ Technology will continue to drive the advancement of knowledge.
- ◆ Use of multidisciplinary teams will facilitate integration of data from various sources.
- ◆ Increased understanding of human movement will help professionals design solutions to remediate problems for people of all ages and abilities.
- ◆ More research on women and the elderly?

Chapter 7: Exercise Physiology and Fitness

◆ What is exercise physiology?

◆ What is the role of physical activity and exercise in achieving physical fitness and health?

◆ How do you use the FITT formula to design a fitness program?

◆ What are the contributors and deterrents to fitness?

Exercise Physiology

◆ The study of the effects of exercise on the body.

◆ Body's responses and adaptations to exercises
  ↗ System to subcellular level
  ↗ Acute (short term) to chronic (long term) adaptations

◆ Population served
  ↗ Elite performer
  ↗ People of all ages and abilities

Historical Development

◆ Specialized area of study mid 1960s and 1970s.

◆ Late 1800s, the use of anthropometry to measure changes in students' development after training programs.

◆ McKenzie: Investigating effects of exercise on various systems of the body and the idea of preventative medicine (early 1900s)

◆ After WWII: increased interest in fitness as a result of youth fitness tests and the results of the physicals of men in the military.

Historical Development

- **1970s**: American Physiological Society recognized exercise physiology as a specialized area of physiology.
- **1974**: ACSM: *Guidelines for Graded Exercise Testing and Prescription*
- **1980s and 1990s**: Understanding of the relationship between physical activity and health.
  - ↗ 1996: **Physical Activity and Health** A REPORT OF THE SURGEON GENERAL
- **2000**: 1st certification exams for *Clinical Exercise Physiologists*
- *Healthy People 2010*

Areas of Study

- Effects of various exercises on various systems of the body
- Relationship of energy metabolism to performance
- Effectiveness of training programs
- Effects of environmental factors
- Effects of individual differences on fitness development and performance

Areas of Study

- Identification of factors that limit performance
- Effectiveness of various rehabilitation programs
- Ergogenic aids and exercise
- Health and therapeutic effects associated with exercise
- Effects of nutrition on performance

Specialization

◆ **Cardiac rehabilitation**
  ↗ Assessment of cardiovascular functioning
  ↗ Prevention of cardiovascular disease
  ↗ Rehabilitation of individuals with the disease
◆ **Exercise biochemistry**
  ↗ Effects of exercise at the cellular level
  ↗ **Exercise epidemiology**: Relationship between physical activity and mortality
  ↗ **Pediatric exercise science**:Scientific study of the response of the body to exercise during childhood and maturation.

Physical Fitness

◆ Ability of the body's systems to function efficiently and effectively.
◆ One is "**physically fit**" if they have the ability to:
  ↗ "carry out daily tasks with vigor and alertness, without undue fatigue, and with ample energy to enjoy leisure-time pursuits and to meet unforeseen emergencies."

Physical Fitness

◆ Health fitness
  ↗ Body composition
  ↗ Cardiorespiratory endurance
  ↗ Flexibility
  ↗ Muscular endurance
  ↗ Muscular strength

◆ Performance or skill-related fitness
  ↗ Agility
  ↗ Balance
  ↗ Coordination
  ↗ Power
  ↗ Reaction Time
  ↗ Speed

Physical Activity, Physical Fitness, and Health

- ◆ Hypokinetic diseases
  - ↗ Diseases caused by insufficient physical activity, often in conjunction with inappropriate dietary practices.
- ◆ Dose-response debate
  - ↗ What kind of activity?
  - ↗ How much time spent in activity?
  - ↗ At what intensity should it be performed?
  - ↗ How often in order to see benefits?

Physical Activity and Health

- ◆ 1996: **Physical Activity and Health** A REPORT OF THE SURGEON GENERAL :
  - ↗ "Individuals who engage in moderate intensity exercise for at least 30 minutes for most, or preferably all, days of the week, can improve their health and decrease their risk for disease."
- ◆ Additional health benefits can be derived from increasing the time and/or intensity of physical activity.
- ◆ It's never too late to be active!

Health Benefits

- ◆ Enhanced cardiovascular function
- ◆ Reduction of many cardiovascular disease risk factors
- ◆ Increase ability to perform tasks of daily living
- ◆ Reduced risk of muscle and joint injury
- ◆ Improved work performance
- ◆ Improved physical appearance, self-image, and sound mental health

Health Benefits

- Reduction of susceptibility to depression and anxiety
- Management of stress
- Enhancement of self-concept and esteem
- Socialization through participation in physical activities
- Improved overall general motor performance
- Energy
- Resistance to fatigue
- Mitigate the debilitating effects of old-age or retain a more desirable level of health for a longer period of time

Energy Production for Physical Activity

- Use of ATP as energy to perform muscular activity. Two ways to produce ATP:
- Anaerobic system
  - ↗ Without oxygen
  - ↗ High energy expenditure, short time (6-60 seconds)
- Aerobic system
  - ↗ With oxygen
  - ↗ Lower rate of energy expenditure, longer period of time (more than 3 minutes)

Principles of Fitness Training

- **Principle of overload**
  - ↗ To improve, one must perform more than one's normal amount of exercise.
- **Principle of specificity**
  - ↗ Programs should be designed in relation to specific goals in mind.
- **Individual's initial fitness level**
  - ↗ Assess initial level of fitness to design realistic program and a starting point.
- **Progression of program**
  - ↗ Increase program as individual becomes adjusted.

Principles of Fitness Training

◆ **Individual differences**
  ↗ Individual's work, diet, lifestyle, and management of stress should be taken into consideration.
◆ **Warm-up, workout, cooldown components**
  ↗ Helps prevent injury and prepares body for exercise as well as returns it to a normal state.
◆ **Safety**
  ↗ Information collected from medical screening, and informing individual of environmental conditions
◆ **Behavioral factors**
  ↗ Motivation of individual to adhere to fitness program

Planning a Fitness Program

◆ Threshold of training
  ↗ Minimal level of exercise needed to achieve desired benefits.
◆ Target zone
  ↗ Defines the upper limits of training and the optimal level of exercise.
◆ FITT formula
  ↗ Frequency, Intensity, Time, and Type
  ↗ Manipulate these factors to produce an individualized exercise program.
◆ Needs and goals of individual
  ↗ Program should meet the goals of the individual

FITT formula

◆ Frequency
  ↗ Number of sessions each week
◆ Intensity
  ↗ Degree of effort put forth by the individual during exercise.
◆ Time
  ↗ Duration of activity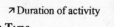
◆ Type
  ↗ Mode of exercise being performed

Cardiorespiratory Endurance

- Body's ability to deliver oxygen effectively to the working muscles to perform physical activity.
- Most important component of health fitness.
- Helps prevent hypokinetic disease.
- Concerned with the aerobic efficiency of the body.

Cardiorespiratory Endurance

- Frequency: 3 to 5 times per week
- Intensity: 60% to 90% HR_{MAX}
- Time: 20 - 30 minutes
- Type: Aerobic activities
  - Jogging
  - Running
  - Walking
  - Dancing
  - Cross Country Skiing
  - Biking
  - Swimming

Target Zone

- HR_{MAX}=220 bpm - age
- Target zone = 60% to 90% HR_{MAX}
- Lower threshold target HR= HR_{MAX} x 60%
- Upper threshold target HR= HR_{MAX} x 90%
- Calculations for a 20-year-old
  - HR_{MAX} =220-20=200 bpm
  - Lower threshold = 200 bpm x 60%=120 bpm
  - Upper threshold = 200 bpm x 90%=180 bpm

Body Composition

- Percentage of body weight composed of fat as compared with fat-free or lean tissue.
  - ↗ Determined by height and weight tables or BMI
- Obesity is associated with numerous health problems and earlier mortality.
  - ↗ In 1999, and estimated 61% of adults were either overweight or obese, and 13% of children were overweight.
- Determination of the cause of obesity is important.

Body Composition

- Body composition is primarily influenced by nutrition and physical activity.
- Energy balance is important to achieving a favorable body composition.
- Energy expenditure through:
  - ↗ **basal metabolism** (maintenance of essential life functions)
  - ↗ **work** (including exercise)
  - ↗ **excretion** of body wastes

Body Composition

Percent Body Fat

	Male	Female
Average	18%	23%
Desirable	12% or less	18% or less
Lower limit	3%	12%

Classifications for BMI

Classification	BMI
Underweight	<18.5 kg/m²
Normal weight	18.5 - 24.9 kg/m²
Overweight	25 - 29.9 kg/m²
Obesity (Class 1)	30 - 34.9 kg/m²
Obesity (Class 2)	35 - 39.9 kg/m²
Extreme Obesity (Class 3)	≥ 40 kg/m²

Energy Balance

- Number of calories taken into the body as food
  -Number of calories expended

  Energy or caloric balance
- Caloric expenditure
  - ↗ Neutral balance
    - » Caloric intake equals expenditure.
  - ↗ Positive balance
    - » More calories consumed than expended.
  - ↗ Negative balance
    - » More calories are expended than consumed.

Body Composition Improvement

- ◆ Decreasing percentage of fat
  - ↗ Decrease caloric intake through diet.
  - ↗ Increase caloric expenditure through physical activity and exercise.
  - ↗ Moderate decrease in caloric intake and moderate increase in caloric expenditure.
- ◆ Follow sound practices
  - ↗ Obsession with weight loss, in conjunction with many other factors, **may** contribute to the development of an eating disorder.

Measurement of Body Composition

- ◆ Hydrostatic weighing
- ◆ Skinfold measurements
  - ↗ Skinfold caliper from selected sites ➔
  - ↗ Use of formulas to calculate percentage of body fat
- ◆ Body mass index (BMI)
  - ↗ height-to-weight ratio

Anorexia Nervosa

- Intense fear of fatness
- Altered perception of body image
- Weight loss of 15% or more below minimal normal body weight
- Obsession with losing increasing amounts of weight
- Increasing preoccupation with food
- Severe food restriction

Anorexia Nervosa

- Increased physical activity and excessive exercising
- Lack of sexual desire, in females absence of menstrual periods
- Changes in mood - irritability, anxiety, and depression
- No known physical or psychological illness that can account for weight loss

Bulimia

- Recurrent episodes of binge eating
- Inconspicuous eating
- Binge episode ended by abdominal pain, sleep, or self-induced vomiting
- Feelings of loss of control when vomiting
- Food restriction to lose weight when not bingeing

Bulimia

- ◆ Vomiting, fasting, exercising, or laxative abuse
- ◆ Fear of not being able to stop eating voluntarily
- ◆ Frequent weight fluctuations greater than 10 pounds
- ◆ Depressed mood following bingeing

_____

_____

_____

_____

_____

 ## Muscular Strength and Endurance

- ◆ Muscular strength is the ability of a muscle or a muscle group to exert a single force against a resistance.
- ◆ Muscular endurance is the ability of a muscle or muscle group to exert force repeatedly or over a period of time.
- ◆ Maintenance of proper posture; protect joints.
- ◆ Production of power to enhance performance.
- ◆ Use it of lose it!

_____

_____

_____

_____

_____

Exercises

- ◆ Isometric exercises
  - ↗ Muscle exerts force against an immovable object.
  - ↗ Static contraction
- ◆ Isotonic exercises
  - ↗ Force is generated while the muscle is changing in length.
  - ↗ Concentric and Eccentric contractions
- ◆ Isokinetic exercises
  - ↗ Contractions are performed at a constant velocity.
  - ↗ Cybex and Orthotron machines

_____

_____

_____

_____

_____

Development of Muscular Strength and Endurance

- ◆ Principle of **Overload** is critical.
- ◆ **Repetition** is the performance of a movement through the full range of motion.
- ◆ **Set** is the number of repetitions of performed without rest.
- ◆ **Strength**
  - ↗ Low number of repetitions with a heavy resistance.
- ◆ **Endurance**
  - ↗ High number of repetitions with a low resistance.
- ◆ **FITT**

 ## Flexibility

- ◆ Maximum range of motion possible at a joint
- ◆ <u>Joint specific</u>: better range of motion in some joints than in others.
- ◆ Can prevent muscle injuries; improve low-back pain
- ◆ <u>Decreased flexibility</u> can be caused by:
  - ↗ Sedentary lifestyle (lack of use of muscles)
  - ↗ Age
  - ↗ High amounts of body fat
  - ↗ Stress

 ## Flexibility

- ◆ **Improvement** of flexibility
  - ↗ **Ballistic** stretching
    - » Momentum generated from repeated bouncing to stretch.
    - » Not recommended- may overstretch the muscle.
  - ↗ **Static** stretching
    - » Slowly moving into a stretching position and holding for a certain period of time (10-30 seconds; 5 times).
  - ↗ **Contract-relax** technique
    - » Relaxing of the muscle to be stretched by contracting the opposite muscle (hamstrings/quadriceps)
- ◆ **Measurement** of flexibility-goniometer

Conducting Fitness Programs

◆ Provide for cognitive and affective goals as well as physical activity.
◆ Make fitness enjoyable.
◆ Establish goals and a plan of action to attain them.
◆ Monitor progress.
◆ Provide for maintenance of fitness.
◆ Fitness requires personal commitment.

Effects of Training

☑ Lower oxygen consumption
☑ Lower pulse rate
☑ Larger stroke volume
☑ Lower rise in blood pressure
☑ Slower respiration rate
☑ Lower rate of lactic acid formation
☑ Faster return to "normal"

Effects of Training

☑ Greater cardiorespiratory efficiency.
☑ Greater endurance.
☑ More "work" can be performed at less cost.
☑ Improvement in fitness components.
☑ Coordination and timing of movements are better.

Physical Activity & Health

- Adults - 30 minutes of physical activity equal to brisk walking on most, preferably all, days of the week.
- Activity of greater intensity will yield greater health benefits.
- Strength-developing activities at least twice a week.

Environmental Considerations

- Hot and humid weather
  - Use extreme caution
  - Heat cramps, heat exhaustion, heat stroke
  - Fluid replacement
  - Adaptation
- Extreme cold weather

  - Heat conservation
  - Hypothermia
  - Frostbite

Myths about Exercise and Weight Control

- Exercise burns relatively few calories.
- Exercise increases the appetite.
- Exercise can be used for spot-reducing.
- Passive exercise machines are not effective.
- Improper weight-loss approaches.

Nutrition and Fitness

◆ Nutrients
  - ↗ carbohydrates
  - ↗ fats
  - ↗ proteins
  - ↗ vitamins
  - ↗ minerals
  - ↗ water
◆ Maintaining water balance is important.
◆ A well-balanced diet is necessary to obtain all the nutrients required by the body.

Nutrition

◆ Food pyramid offers guidelines for eating a balanced diet.
◆ Current U.S. diet is too high in fat, cholesterol, sugar, and sodium and lacking in carbohydrates and fiber.
◆ Carefully monitor caloric intake **AND** caloric expenditure.
◆ Special diets for special situations.

Dietary Guidelines for Americans, 2000

◆ Aim For Fitness
  - ↗ Aim for a healthy weight.
  - ↗ Be physically active each day.
◆ Build A Healthy Base
  - ↗ Let the Pyramid guide your food choices.
  - ↗ Eat a variety of grains, fruits, and vegetables daily.
  - ↗ Keep food safe to eat.
◆ Choose Sensibly
  - ↗ Choose a diet low in saturated fat, cholesterol, and moderate in total fat.
  - ↗ Choose beverages and foods to moderate intake of sugars.
  - ↗ Choose and prepare foods with less salt.
  - ↗ Drink alcoholic beverages in moderation.

Stress Management

- ◆ **Stress** is the body's physiological response to demands placed on it.
- ◆ Nature of **stressors** (physical or cognitive)
- ◆ Nature of stress response ("fight or flight")
- ◆ The critical role of perception in interpretation and management of stress
- ◆ Stress and its role in disease
  - ↗ Coronary heart disease, cancer, hypertension, eating disorders, depression, etc.

Stress Management

- ◆ Use stress to your advantage
- ◆ Approaches to manage stress
  - ↗ Relaxation training
  - ↗ Physical activity
  - ↗ Cognitive strategies
  - ↗ Time management
  - ↗ Biofeedback
- ◆ Physical fitness contributes to stress resistance

Deterrents to Fitness

- ◆ Dietary practices
- ◆ Tobacco
- ◆ Excessive alcohol consumption
- ◆ Use of drugs
- ◆ Inappropriate stress management approaches

Tobacco and Fitness

- Over 430,000 premature deaths/ year are related to smoking.
- 25% of adults smoke.
- Children and teens constitute 90% of the new smokers.
- Average age of starting is 13.
- Second hand smoke contributes to 3,000 deaths of nonsmokers each year.
- Significant role in all cancers.
- Detracts from fitness

 ## Drug Abuse

- Use of an illicit drug or use of a legal drug in a manner that is harmful to health and well-being.
- Psychoactive drugs are most frequently abused.
  - ⊅ Those that alter one's behaviors, feelings, and perceptions.
- Development of dependence.
- Health risks associated with drug abuse.
- Death as a result of overdose of severe reaction.

Alcohol and Fitness

- Impact of alcohol on physical and psychological state, therefore it is a drug.
- Alcoholism is a serious disease affecting more than 10 million Americans.
  - ⊅ Liver damage, cardiovascular disease
  - ⊅ CNS impairment, malnutrition
  - ⊅ Fetal Alcohol Syndrome
  - ⊅ Negatively affects one's body composition

Chapter 8: Sociological Foundations of Physical Education and Sport

- How is sport a socializing force in American culture?
- What is the nature and scope of sport?
- What are some problems that we see today in sports and how are they addressed?

Sociology

- Study of people, groups, institutions, human activities in terms of social behavior, and social order within society.
- Concerned about institutions in society such as religion, family, government, education, and leisure.

Sociology

- Influence of social institutions on the individual, the social behavior and human relations that occur within a group or an institution, and how they influence the individual, and the interrelationship between various institutions within society, such as sport, education, religion, and government.

Sport Sociology

◆ Examination of the relationship between sport and society.

◆ **Goals of Sport Sociology** (Coakley)
  ↗ Factors underlying the creation and the organization of sports.
  ↗ Relationship between sport and other aspects of society such as family, education, and the media.
  ↗ Influence of sport and sport participation on individuals' beliefs relative to equity, gender, race, ethnicity, disability, and other societal issues.
  ↗ The social dynamics within the sport setting, i.e., organizational structure, group actions, and interaction patterns.
  ↗ The influence of cultural, structural, and situational factors on the nature of sport and the sport experience.
  ↗ The social processes associated with sport, including competition, socialization, conflict, and change.

Historical Development

◆ Distinct field of inquiry in the late 1960s.

◆ Veblen wrote *The Theory of the Leisure Class* (1899), critiquing sport practices.

◆ Both *Sports in American Life (1953)* and *Man, Play, and Games (1961)* analyzed the role of play in culture.

◆ 1964: International Committee of Sport Sociology which later became known as International Sociology of Sport Association (ISSA) in 1994.

Historical Development

◆ Journals
  ↗ *International Review of Sport Sociology* became known as *International Review for the Sociology of Sport* (1984).
  ↗ *Journal of Sport and Social Issues* (1977)
  ↗ *Sociology of Sport Journal* (1984)

Historical Development

- ◆ Topics that have gotten the most attention are those related to social inequalities:
  - ↗ Gender, race, ethnicity, wealth, sexual orientation, and culture
- ◆ **1970s** focused on socioeconomic inequalities and class relations in sport.
- ◆ **1980s** focused on class and gender inequities in sport.
- ◆ **1990s** focused on exercise and societal conceptions of the body, racial and ethnic inequities, the impact of the media and politics on sport in different cultures.

What does a sport sociologist do?

- ◆ Studies the behavior of individuals and groups within the sport milieu.
- ◆ Influence of social relationships, past social experiences, and the social setting of sport activities on the behavior of groups and individuals in sport.

Sport sociology questions...

- ◆ Does sport build character?
- ◆ Does sport help minorities become more fully integrated into society?
- ◆ How do the mass media affect sport?
- ◆ How does youth sport influence children's lives?
- ◆ How are politics and sports interrelated?
- ◆ How does sport influence athletes' academic achievements?

SPORT

◆ "Sports are institutionalized competitive activities that involve rigorous physical exertion or the use of relatively complex physical skills by participants motivated by personal enjoyment and external rewards."

　　　　　　　　-Coakley

◆ Do you agree with this definition of sport? Why or why not?

Characteristics of Sport

◆ What kind of activities can be classified as sport?

◆ Under what circumstances can participation in activities be considered sport?

◆ What characterizes the involvement of participants in sport?

What sport does for people...

◆ Emotional release
◆ Affirmation of identity
◆ Social control
◆ Socialization
◆ Agent for change
◆ Collective conscious
◆ Success

Sport in the Educational Institutions

♦ Rapid period of growth starting with the first collegiate athletic event in 1852, a crew race between Harvard and Yale.

♦ Introduction and growth of sports at collegiate and interscholastic levels.

♦ Concerns voiced about the educational value of sports. What's more important: the academics or the athletics?

Interscholastic Sports

♦ Sports contribution to educational goals.

♦ Arguments for and against interscholastic sports.

♦ Concerns
  ↗ **Overemphasis on Winning**
    » Pressure to specialize in one sport and win instead of participating in many.
  ↗ **Restriction of Opportunities for Students**
    » Only limited number of students can participate due to limited resources.
  ↗ **Eligibility Requirements**: Are there any academic standards?

Interscholastic sports

♦ Concerns
  ↗ **Drug Abuse**
    » Use of performance-enhancing drugs mainly anabolic steriods, and creatine.
  ↗ **Soaring Costs**
    » "Pay to Play": those that have the money can afford to play, but others lose out if required to pay.
  ↗ **Quality of the Leadership**
    » Educational goals go unmet in instances of verbal abuse and control of the athletes' lives by the coach.
    » Do coaches have to be certified?

Intercollegiate Sport

- ◆ **Educational Sport -vs- "Big Business"**
- ◆ **Governance**
  - ↗ NCAA, NAIA, NJCAA
- ◆ **Pressures to win**
  - ↗ Usually result in the abandonment of sportsmanship, character and social development
- ◆ **Academic achievement of "student-athletes"**
  - ↗ Graduation rates
  - ↗ Proposition 48 and subsequent rulings
- ◆ **Exploitation of athletes**
  - ↗ Athletes can make millions for their school, and only receive a full scholarship in return.

Intercollegiate Athletics

- ◆ **Gambling**
  - ↗ $2.5 billion was illegally wagered on the NCAA Div. I Men's Basketball Championship.
- ◆ **Retention of Coaches**
- ◆ **Drug abuse**
  - ↗ Pressure to win and the use of performance-enhancing drugs.
- ◆ **Spiraling costs**
- ◆ **Media**
  - ↗ Had brought to light many illegal recruiting practices.

Intercollegiate Athletics Reform

- ◆ In1990, athletes' graduation rates were required to be monitored.
- ◆ Elimination of athletic dormitories.
- ◆ Reduction of time allowed in practice/week, and the length of the season.
- ◆ Can we fix the resemblance to the professional model of sports or is it too late?

Concerns in Sports Today <small>(Michner)</small>

- ◆ Discrimination against girls and women.
- ◆ Children's programs place too much emphasis on winning.
- ◆ Children engaged in highly competitive sport at too early an age.
- ◆ Money spent by "big-time" collegiate sport is excessive.
- ◆ Recruitment of high school athletes is often scandalous.
- ◆ Television threatens to destroy many of sports' values.
- ◆ Violence in sports is excessive.
- ◆ Public support of professional sport is questionable.

Girls and Women in Sports

- ◆ **Title IX** of the Educational Amendment Act 1972
  - ↗ "no person ... shall on the basis of sex, be excluded form participation in, be denied the benefits of or be subjected to discrimination under any educational program or activity receiving federal assistance."
- ◆ Challenges to Title IX (narrow interpretation)
  - ↗ Grove City College Vs. Bell
- ◆ 1988 Civil Rights Restoration Act (broad)
  - ↗ Demanded equal opportunity for both sexes in all programs in any organization that received federal funds.

Girls and Women in Sport

- ◆ Compliance with Title IX
  - ↗ Proportionality
  - ↗ History and continued practice
  - ↗ Accommodation of interests and abilities
- ◆ Impact of Title IX
  - ↗ Interscholastic sports
  - ↗ Intercollegiate sports
    - » Increases in number of teams, scholarships offered, and qualified coaches hired

Physical Activity and Sport in the Lives of Girls (1997)

◆ Exercise and sport participation ...
  ↗ **contributes to the development of the "complete" girl ...**
    » her social, physical, emotional, and cultural environment
      -- rather than to one aspect of the girl's life.
  ↗ **a therapeutic and preventive intervention to enhance the
    physical and mental health.**
  ↗ **enhances the mental health of girls through
    opportunities to develop positive feelings about their
    body, improved self-esteem, tangible experiences of
    competency and success, and enhanced self-confidence**

Physical Activity and Sport in the
Lives of Girls (1997)

◆ Sports contribute to educational goals.
◆ Poverty substantially limits many girls'
  access to physical activity and sport.
◆ The potential for girls to derive positive
  experiences from physical activity and sport
  is limited by lack of opportunity and
  stereotypes.

Girls and Women in Sports

◆ Expansion of opportunities for girls and women due to:
  ↗ **increased visibility of women athlete role models**
  ↗ **fitness movement**
  ↗ **women's movement**
  ↗ **legislation**
◆ Factors limiting participation
  ↗ financial constraints
  ↗ societal constraints
  ↗ discrimination

Girls and Women in Sport

- ◆ Women in the Olympics
  - ↗ Women have fewer events and participants than men.
    - » In 1972, U.S. team 342 men and 96 women.
    - » In 1996, U.S. team 382 men and 280 women.
  - ↗ 1996 women made up 36.5% of the athletes.
  - ↗ IOC slow to approve new events for women even though women are participating in world competition in these events.

Girls and Women in Sport

- ◆ Female Coaches
  - ↗ Since passage of Title IX, the number of female coaches has declined.
  - ↗ Decline of female intercollegiate coaches
    - » In 1970, 90% of coaches of female teams were women.
    - » In 2000, 42.2% of coaches of female teams were women.
  - ↗ Reasons for underrepresentation are varied.
    - » Lack of well qualified women coaches and administrators.
    - » Lack of visibility of women as role models in these careers.

Girls and Women in Sport

- ◆ Media
  - ↗ Trivialization of females' accomplishments
  - ↗ Lack of coverage
  - ↗ Reinforcement of traditional stereotypes
- ◆ Myths
  - ↗ Participation leads to complications in childbearing.
  - ↗ Women more likely to be insured.
  - ↗ Participation threatens one's femininity.

Minorities in Sport

- ◆ Racism and prejudice in sport...
  - ↗ Is sport "color blind"?
- ◆ Integration of sports
  - ↗ 1946, Jackie Robinson became the first African-American to play professional baseball for the Dodgers.
- ◆ Participation patterns of minorities
  - ↗ Black athletes' participation concentrated in a few sports.
- ◆ Underrepresentation of minorities in certain sports and sport administration.

Minorities in Sport

- ◆ **Stacking** is the phenomenon where players from certain racial or ethnic groups are disproportionately represented at certain positions.
  - ↗ A reflection of stereotypical beliefs about racial and ethnic groups?
  - ↗ No consensus as to the causes of stacking.
- ◆ **Other problems**:
  - ↗ Disparity in treatment by coaches
  - ↗ Sacrifice of educational goals for athletic goals
  - ↗ Social isolation
  - ↗ Prejudiced attitudes held by coaches and teammates

Minorities in Sport

- ◆ Native Americans
  - ↗ Limited participation by Native Americans in sports.
  - ↗ Factors that serve to limit participation:
    - » Poverty
    - » Poor health
    - » Lack of equipment
    - » Concern for loss of cultural identity
  - ↗ Use of Native-Americans as mascots is often a reflection of stereotypical beliefs.

Sport for Individuals with Disabilities

◆ Prior to the 1970s, individuals with disabilities had limited opportunities for participation in sport.

◆ Expansion of sports opportunities
  ↗ Changing societal attitudes
  ↗ Use of sport for rehabilitation
  ↗ Federal legislation

Sports for Individuals with Disabilities

◆ Federal legislation
  ↗ **PL 94-142 Education for All Handicapped Children Act**
  ↗ **PL 93-112 Section 504 Rehabilitation Act**
  ↗ **Amateur Sports Act of 1978 PL 95-606**
    » USOC Committee on Sports for the Disabled
    » Recognition of amateur sports organizations for the disabled
    » Paralympics
      ◆ 2000 Paralympic Games in Sydney involved more than 4,000 athletes, competing in 18 sports for 550 medals.

Sport for Children and Youth

◆ Youth sports have grown tremendously.
◆ Widespread concern about the nature and outcomes associated with the programs.
◆ Benefits associated with participation have long been heralded.
◆ Many of the criticisms stem from the overemphasis on winning.
◆ National Alliance for Youth Sports (NAYS)

Sport for Children and Youth

- Leadership is a critical factor in governing the outcomes associated with youth sports.
- Need to structure youth sports to include elements that children find enjoyable within their own games.
- Training of volunteers
- Developmental vs Professional model
- National Alliance for Youth Sports (NAYS)

International Sport: The Olympics

- Olympic ideals are lofty goals due to:
  - Olympics used to further political goals by some
  - Media coverage
  - Nationalism undermining the goal of unity
  - Increased commercialization of the Games
  - Amateurism vs professionalism
- Restructuring of Games to attain goals in the future? How?

Amateur Sport

- Amateur Athletic Union
- State Games
- US Olympic Festival

- Amateur competitions for adults
  - Senior Games
  - Master's competitions

Violence in Sport

- Overextension of physical and psychological intimidation of opponents.
- Bench clearing "brawls" in sports
- **"Enforcers"** on some teams
  - Individuals on a team charged with protecting their own players by intimidating the opponents.
- Violence at the upper levels of sports influences actions of children and youth at lower levels of sport with the help of the media glamorizing it.
- Spectator violence and parental violence

Dealing with Violence in Sport

- No single, simple solution.
- How violent is too violent? Where do you draw the line?
- Some type of control must be instituted.
- Stricter penalties should be imposed at all levels of sport?
- Playing within the spirit of the game and rules, and respecting opponents will reduce violence?

Chapter 9: Psychological Foundations of Physical Education and Sport

◆ What is the information-processing model of motor learning and the concepts related to it?

◆ How do the concepts of feedback, design of practice, and transfer apply to physical education, exercise science, and sport?

◆ What are the psychological benefits of participation in sport and physical activities?

Learning

◆ **Learning** is a relatively permanent change in behavior or performance as a result of instruction, experiences, study, and/or practice.

◆ Learning is inferred from changes in performance.

◆ **Motor behavior** is concerned with the learning or acquisition of skills across the lifespan and encompasses three areas:
  ↗ **Motor learning**
  ↗ **Motor control**
  ↗ **Motor development**

Motor Behavior

◆ **Motor learning**
  ↗ Study of the acquisition of skills as a consequence of practice.

◆ **Motor control**
  ↗ Study of the neural mechanisms and processes by which movements are learned and controlled.

Historical Development of Motor Learning and Motor Control

- ◆ **Early Period** (1880-1940)
    - ↗ Research focused on how did mind worked, not the production of skills.
    - ↗ Thorndike: *Law of Effect*
        - » When responses were rewarded, the behavior strengthened.
- ◆ **Middle Period** (1940-1970)
    - ↗ Craik focused research on how the brain processes and uses information to determine the motor response.
    - ↗ Henry:
        - » "Memory drum theory" (role of cognitive activity in motor learning)

Historical Development of Motor Learning and Motor Control

- ◆ **Present Period** (1970-present)
    - ↗ Emergence of motor learning and motor control within physical education programs.
    - ↗ Closed Loop theory (Adams)
    - ↗ Schema theory (Schmidt)
    - ↗ Dynamical Systems theory (Kelso)

Areas of Study

- ◆ How does the type and frequency of feedback impact skill acquisition?
- ◆ How does the structure of practice influence the retention of skills?
- ◆ What can be done to facilitate the transfer of previous learning to the learning of new skills?
- ◆ How does the aging process affect motor control?
- ◆ How do differences in individuals' learning styles influence their ability to learn motor skills?

Information Processing Model

- **Input**
  - ↗ Information from the environment through the senses.
- **Decision-making**
  - ↗ Input evaluation and integration with past information .
  - ↗ Response selection
- **Output**
  - ↗ Response execution
- **Feedback**
  - ↗ Information about the performance and quality of the movement. Information gained here can guide future interpretations, decisions, and responses.

Stages of Learning

- **Cognitive Stage**
  - ↗ Understanding of the nature and goal of the activity to be learned
  - ↗ Initial attempts at the skill - gross errors
- **Associative Stage**
  - ↗ Practice on mastering the timing of the skill
  - ↗ Fewer and more consistent errors
- **Autonomous Stage**
  - ↗ Well coordinated and appears effortless
  - ↗ Few errors
  - ↗ "Automatic" performance allows attention to be directed to other aspects of skill performance

Factors Influencing Learning

- **Readiness**
  - ↗ Physiological and psychological factors influencing an individual's ability and willingness to learn.
- **Motivation**
  - ↗ A condition within an individual that initiates activity directed toward a goal. (Needs and drives are necessary.)
- **Reinforcement**
  - ↗ Using events, actions, and behaviors to increase the likelihood of a certain response recurring. May be positive or negative
- **Individual differences**
  - ↗ Backgrounds, abilities, intelligence, learning styles, and personalities of students

Ten Motor Learning Concepts

1. Practice sessions should be structured to promote optimal conditions for learning.
2. Learners must understand the task to be learned.
3. The nature of the skill or task to be learned should be considered when designing practice.
4. Whether to teach by the whole or the part method depends on the nature of the skill and the learner
5. Whether speed or accuracy should be emphasized in teaching a skill depends on the requirements of the skill.

Ten Motor Learning Concepts

6. Transfer of learning can facilitate the acquisition of motor skills.
7. Feedback is essential for learning.
   ⬈ Knowledge of results (KR)
   ⬈ Knowledge of performance (KP)
8. Learners may experience plateaus in learning.
9. Self-analysis should be developed.
10. Leadership influences the amount of learning.

Motor Development

◆ Study of the origins and changes in movement behavior throughout the lifespan.
◆ Biological and environmental influences on motor behavior from infancy to old age.
◆ Influence of psychological, sociological, cognitive, biological, and mechanical factors on motor behavior.
◆ Rate and sequence of development.

Historical Development

- ◆ **Maturational Period** (1928-1946)
  - ↗ Research on the underlying biological processes guiding maturation.
  - ↗ The rate and sequences of motor *development* from infancy in terms of acquisition of rudimentary and mature movements.
- ◆ **Normative/Descriptive Period** (1946-1970s)
  - ↗ Description of the motor *performances* of children.
  - ↗ Research on how growth and maturation affect performance and the impact of perceptual-motor development.
- ◆ **Process-Oriented Period** (1980s-present)
  - ↗ Research on how cognitive factors influence motor skill acquisition and motor development based on dynamical systems theory.

Areas of Study

- ◆ What are the heredity and environmental factors most significantly associated with obesity?
- ◆ At what age can children safely engage in resistance training?
- ◆ How does socioeconomic status affect the development of motor skills?
- ◆ How does early sensory stimulation affect the development of motor skills?
- ◆ What are the changes in motor skill development experienced across the lifespan?

Phases of Motor Development

- ◆ Gallahue developed an hourglass model…
- ◆ **Early reflexive and rudimentary** movement phases:
  - ↗ Hereditary is the primary factor for development. Sequential progression of development but individuals' rates of development will differ.
- ◆ **Fundamental** movement phase:
  - ↗ Skill acquisition based on encouragement, instruction, and opportunities for practice.
- ◆ **Specialized** movement phase: Refinement of skills
- ◆ **"Turnover":** Hereditary and environmental factors that influence the rate of the aging process.

Fundamental Movement Phase

- ◆ **Initial Stage** (~ age 2)
  - ↗ Poor spatial and temporal integration of skill movements.
  - ↗ Improper sequencing of the parts of the skill
  - ↗ Poor rhythm, difficulties in coordination
- ◆ **Elementary Stage** (~ age 3 & 4)
  - ↗ Greater control and rhythmical coordination
  - ↗ Temporal and spatial elements are better synchronized.
  - ↗ Movements are still restricted, exaggerated, or inconsistent.
- ◆ **Mature Stage** (~age 5 or 6)
  - ↗ Increased efficiency, enhanced coordination, and improved control of movements.
  - ↗ Greater force production

Psychology of Sport and Exercise

- ◆ "The systematic scholarly study of the behavior, feelings, and thoughts of people engaged in sport, exercise, and physical activity." (Vealey)
- ◆ Questions addressed:
  - ↗ Is the personality profile of an elite athlete ?
  - ↗ What are the psychological benefits of participation in regular physical activity?
  - ↗ How does anxiety influence performance?
  - ↗ What factors influence an individual's adherence to a rehabilitation program?
  - ↗ How does self-confidence influence performance?

Historical Development

- ◆ **Late 1890s and early 1900s**: Norman Triplett did first research on what became known as the Social Facilitation Theory.

- ◆ **1918**: Griffith known as the "father of sport psychology"
  - ↗ In 1938, he became the Chicago Cubs team's sport psychologist researching how to enhance motivation and improve self-confidence.

- ◆ **Late 1960s and 1970s:**
  - ↗ Sport psychology as a subdiscipline of physical education.
  - ↗ Undergraduate and graduate curriculums, research programs, and professional societies.
  - ↗ 1979: *Journal of Sport Psychology* began publication.

Historical Development

- **1980s:** Researchers embraced an applied approach to the field.
  - ↗ 1986: Association for the Advancement of Applied Sport Psychology (AAASP) was organized.
  - ↗ Exercise psychology evolved as a specialized area of study.
  - ↗ Increase of interest by clinically trained psychologists help to shape the field.
  - ↗ 1988: *Journal of Sport Psychology* became known as *Journal of Sport and Exercise Psychology*
- **1990s-present**
  - ↗ Rich diversity in approaches to the field and areas of study.
  - ↗ Tremendous opportunity to teach, consult, and research in the field.

Psychological Benefits of Physical Activity

- Improves health-related quality of life.
- Improves one's mood.
- Alleviates symptoms associated with mild depression.
- Reduces anxiety.
- Aids in managing stress.
- Enhances self-concept, self-esteem, self-efficacy, and self-confidence.
- Offers opportunities for affiliation with others.

Psychological Benefits of Physical Activity

- Offers opportunities to experience "peak" moments.
- Provides recreation and a change of pace.
- Offers an opportunity for individuals to challenge themselves and strive for mastery.
- Offers creative and aesthetic experiences.
- Increasing recognition of physical activity as a therapeutic modality.

Exercise and Adherence

- ◆ Estimates reveal that nearly 50% of patients fail to comply with their medical treatment.
- ◆ Adherence to supervised exercise programs ranges from 50% to 80%.
- ◆ Only 30% of individuals who begin an exercise program will be exercising at the end of 3 years.
- ◆ What can be done to promote continued involvement?

Exercise and Adherence: Intervention Models

- ◆ Classic learning theories
  - ↗ Learning a new behavior is achieved by altering the many small behaviors that compose the overall behavior.
  - ↗ Break behavior down into smaller goals to be achieved.
  - ↗ Work incrementally toward goal.
  - ↗ Reinforcement is important; provide rewards and incentives (both immediate and long-range).

Exercise and Adherence: Intervention Models

- ◆ Health belief model
  - ↗ Adoption of a health behavior depends on the person's perception of four factors:
    - » Severity of potential illness
    - » Susceptibility to illness
    - » Benefits of taking action
    - » Barriers to action
  - ↗ Self-efficacy is an important component of this model.

Exercise and Adherence: Intervention Models

◆ Social cognitive theory
  ↗ Behavior change is influenced by environmental factors, personal factors, and attributes of the behavior itself.
  ↗ Self-efficacy is central to this model.
  ↗ Individual must believe in his or her ability to perform the behavior and must perceive an incentive for changing the behavior.
  ↗ Outcomes must be valued by the individual.

Exercise and Adherence: Intervention Models

◆ **Transtheoretical model** "stages of change":
  » Precontemplation
  » Contemplation
  » Preparation
  » Action
  » Maintenance
  » Termination
  ↗ Decisional balance (weighing the pros and cons of the change)
  ↗ Self-efficacy (confidence about his/her abilities in a situation)
  ↗ Target the intervention to the individual's current stage.

Exercise and Adherence: Intervention Models

◆ **Ecological approach**
  ↗ Comprehensive approach to health.
  ↗ Development of individual skills is emphasized as well as creating supportive, health-promoting environment.
  ↗ Environmental and societal influences and limitations on health behavior should be considered when planning for behavior change.

Exercise Dropout   EXIT

- Low self-motivation
- Depression
- Low self-efficacy
- Denial of seriousness of one's health condition
- Obesity
- Type A behavior pattern
- Smokers
- Blue-collar workers
- Perception that exercise has few health benefits
- Inactive lifestyle Sedentary occupations
- Lack of social support
- Family problems
- Interference of job-related responsibilities
- Inconvenience
- High-intensity exercise

Exercise Adherence

- Educational approaches
  - Increase participants knowledge and understanding of the benefits of physical activity and exercise.
- Behavioral approaches
  - **Reinforcement**
  - **Contracting**
  - **Self-monitoring**
  - **Goal-setting**
  - **Enhancement of self-efficacy**

Exercise Adherence

- Program Design
  - Increase social support available to participants.
  - Offer programs at convenient times and locations.
  - Goal-setting and periodic assessment.
  - Enthusiastic leaders.
  - Strong communication.
  - Establishment of rapport.
  - Consideration of individual needs and interests.

Rehabilitation Adherence

◆ Strategies to enhance adherence to a rehabilitation program are important for sports medicine programs.

◆ Adherence can be increased by:
  ↗ **Providing social support**
  ↗ **Goal setting**
  ↗ **Effective communication**
  ↗ **Tailoring program to individual needs**
  ↗ **Monitoring progress**
  ↗ **Collaborative approach to accomplishing goals**

Personality

◆ Impact of athletics on personality development.

◆ Relationship between personality and athletic performance.
  ↗ Do athletes differ from nonathletes?
  ↗ Can athletes in certain sports be distinguished from athletes in other sports?
  ↗ Do individuals participate in certain sports because of their personality characteristics?
  ↗ Do highly skilled athletes in a sport have different personality characteristics than the lesser skilled athletes?
  ↗ Can personality predict success in sport?

◆ **Each athlete must be treated as an individual.**

Anxiety and Arousal

◆ **Anxiety** is a subjective feeling of apprehension accompanied by a heightened level of physiological arousal.

◆ **Physiological arousal** is an autonomic response that results in the excitation of various organs of the body.

◆ **Trait and state anxiety**
  ↗ Trait: integral part of an individual's personality.
  ↗ State: emotional response to a specific situation that results in feelings of fear, tension, or apprehension.

◆ Find the optimal level of arousal that allows for peak performance.

Reducing Anxiety

- Use physical activity (warm-ups) to release stress and anxiety.
- Develop precompetition routines.
- Simulate games in practice to rehearse skills and strategies.
- Tailor preparation for the competition to the individual athlete. Each athlete will have different needs.
- Build self-confidence and high, but realistic expectations.
- Keep errors in perspective.

Attention

- Ability to direct senses and thought processes to particular objects, thoughts, and feelings
- **Dimensions of attention**
  - Width: Broad to narrow
  - Direction: External to internal
- **Attentional flexibility**
  - Be able to rapidly switch back and forth between various attentional styles at will, depending on what the task demands.
- Anxiety tends to narrow and internalize attentional focus, and this will impact performance. How?

Intervention Strategies

- <u>WHY?</u> To help athletes achieve optimal performance.
  - **Management of anxiety and arousal**
    - » Relaxation techniques
  - **Cognitive strategies**
    - » Restructuring
    - » Thought stopping
    - » Self-talk
    - » Imagery
  - **Goal setting**

Chapter 10: Career and Professional
Development in Physical Education and Sport

◆Identify career opportunities in physical
education, exercise science, and sport.

◆Be able to self-assess strengths, interests, goals,
and career preferences.

◆Identify leadership skills for professionals in the
field of physical education, exercise science, and
sport.

◆List professional organizations in physical
education, exercise science, and sport.

 Growth of Career Opportunities

◆ Greater societal interest and knowledge
demands a need for competent professionals to
design, lead, and evaluate physical activity
programs.

◆ Changing definition of physical education that
has further developed subdisciplines and the
need for professionals in those areas.

Career Opportunities

◆ **Physical Education and Coaching careers**
  ↗ School and nonschool settings
◆ **Fitness- and Health-related careers**
  ↗ Cardiac Rehabilitation, Sports Nutrition, Corporate Fitness, etc.
◆ **Personal Trainer-Sport Management careers**
  ↗ Athletic Administration, Sport Retailing, Resort Sport
    Management, etc.
◆ **Sport Media careers**
  ↗ Journalism, Photography, Writing, Art, Broadcasting
◆ **Sport-Related careers**
  ↗ Law, Research, Consulting, Officiating, Entrepreneur, etc.

Choosing a Career

◆ **Take some of the anxiety away from choosing a career by thinking about these concepts...**
  ↗ Select a "career pathway" as opposed to a specific job; there are many jobs to pursue within a given career area.
  ↗ A career choice can be changed.
  ↗ A career does not have to be a lifelong commitment.
  ↗ Evaluate your career satisfaction periodically.
  ↗ Know your strengths, interests, goals, and preferences before making a decision.

Career Decision-Making Process

Reflect on your thoughts in these categories before making a decision...
  ↗ Self-assessment of strengths and abilities.
  ↗ Personal and professional goals.
  ↗ Work and lifestyle preferences.
  ↗ Career requirements.

Maximizing Professional Preparation

◆ *Professional preparation* is the attainment of knowledge necessary to be an educated person and that which is essential to understanding the chosen career field. This preparation can take the form of:
◆ Education
  ↗ Practicums
  ↗ Certifications and Professional Courses
  ↗ Personal development
◆ Related experiences
◆ Professional involvement

Transferable Skills

Transferable skills are those skills that have application to many different careers. Some examples are:

- ◆ Speaking
- ◆ Writing
- ◆ Teaching/Instructing
- ◆ Interviewing
- ◆ Public relations
- ◆ Leadership

- ◆ Budget management
- ◆ Negotiating
- ◆ Organizing
- ◆ Computer and analytical skills

Professional Preparation Timetable

A **4-year** timeline focusing on these 10 categories is suggested for individuals concerned with preparing for a professional career.

- ◆ Academic
- ◆ Career goals
- ◆ Campus activities
- ◆ Professional activities
- ◆ Volunteer activities
- ◆ Related work

- ◆ Practicums
- ◆ Career planning
- ◆ Networking
- ◆ Certifications
- ◆ Application
  - ↗ For Employment
  - ↗ For Graduate School

Leadership

- ◆ "The art of influencing people to work together harmoniously to achieve set goals that they endorse."
- ◆ Effective leadership is a skill that can be learned.
- ◆ Interactive nature of leadership---not all leadership characteristics will be necessary in every situation. Know the time and place to lead!
- ◆ Importance of leadership within the field

Leadership Qualities

- ◆ Intelligence
- ◆ Assertion
- ◆ Empathy
- ◆ Intrinsic motivation
- ◆ Flexibility
- ◆ Ambition
- ◆ Self-confidence
- ◆ Optimism

- ◆ Hard work
- ◆ Determination
- ◆ Perseverance
- ◆ Concern for people
- ◆ Respect for others
- ◆ Excellent communication skills
- ◆ Knowledge of the field

(Anshel)

(Weinberg and Gould)

Attributes Of A Skillful Leader

- ◆ Integrity, Trustworthiness
- ◆ Well-defined goals
- ◆ Flexible
- ◆ Self-control
- ◆ Commitment
- ◆ Competence

- ◆ Develops a "vision"
- ◆ Goal Assessment
- ◆ Effective communicator
- ◆ Motivates people
- ◆ Problem-solving skills
- ◆ Opportunistic
- ◆ Courageous

Administrator Skills (McIntyre)

- ◆ **Peer skills**
  - ↗ Establish and foster group and individual peer relationships.
- ◆ **Leadership skills**
  - ↗ Develop a variety of leadership styles, planning skills, performance evaluation skills, and skills to foster positive morale.
- ◆ **Conflict resolution skills**
  - ↗ Learn to deal with group conflict in a positive manner.

Administrator Skills (McIntyre)

- ◆ **Information-processing skills**
  - ↗ Gather and evaluate information, formulate action plans, and disperse information to others.
- ◆ **Decision-making skills**
  - ↗ Identify problem, generate alternative solutions, evaluate possible outcomes of solutions, and select one solution from alternatives.
- ◆ **Introspective skills**
  - ↗ Sensitive to one's behavior and its effects on others.

Principles of Effective Leadership (Mack)

- ◆ Create a vision and commitment.
- ◆ Maintain integrity.
- ◆ Lead by example.
- ◆ Give credit for success and accept responsibility for failure.
- ◆ Praise group contributions.
- ◆ Communicate effectively.
- ◆ Delegate.
- ◆ Practice the Golden Rule.
- ◆ Create an environment for self-motivation.

Leadership Roles (Smith)

- ◆ **Vision role**
  - ↗ Clearly communicate his/her vision to the group.
  - ↗ Create a mission statement and set specific goals contributing to the attainment of the vision.
- ◆ **Relationship role**
  - ↗ Foster relationships that help move toward achievement of the goal.
  - ↗ Team building, and networking to gain support.
- ◆ **Control role**
  - ↗ Prioritize activities to be undertaken and problems to be resolved, as well as determine the resources needed.
  - ↗ Decision-making, delegation, and conflict management.

Leadership Roles (Smith)

- **Encouragement role**
  - ↗ Recognize the contributions of members to the group.
  - ↗ Reinforce efforts through incentives and rewards.
  - ↗ Support actions that move the group towards the goal.
- **Information role**
  - ↗ Maintain channels of communication within the group and the organization.
  - ↗ Make sure members of group have necessary information to fulfill responsibilities.

 ## Professionalism

- Commitment to the field
- Professional competence and conduct
- Possession of required credentials
- Adhere to ethical standards
- Accountability
- Cultural competency
- Enthusiasm
- Interest in new developments
- Leadership skills
- Involvement in further advancement of the field and community
- Personal commitment

Belonging to Professional Organizations Provides...

- Opportunity for service.
- Opportunity to shape the future.
- A channel of communication.
- A means for interpreting the field.
- A source of help and assistance.
- An opportunity for fellowship.
- A forum for research.
- A means for distributing costs.
- Employment opportunities.

AAHPERD

AAHPERD
American Alliance for Health Physical Education Recreation and Dance

- ◆ Established 1885.
- ◆ Committed to developing and maintaining healthy, active lifestyles for all Americans and to enhancing skilled and aesthetic performance.
- ◆ Comprises 6 national organizations:
  - ⊿ AALR, AAHE, AAALF, NAGWS, NASPE, NDA
  - ⊿ Research Consortium
- ◆ Publications:
  - ⊿ *JOPERD, Research Quarterly for Exercise and Sport, Strategies, Update,* and *Health Education*
- ◆ Student Action Council (SAC)

ACSM AMERICAN COLLEGE of SPORTS MEDICINE

- ◆ Founded 1954.
- ◆ Promote and integrate "scientific research, education, and practical applications of sports medicine and exercise science to enhance physical performance, fitness, health, and quality of life."
- ◆ Affiliated with the International Federation of Sports Medicine (IFSM)
- ◆ Publications:
  - ⊿ *Medicine and Science in Sports and Exercise, Sports Medicine Bulletin,* and the *Encyclopedia of Sport Sciences and Medicine.*

NATA National Athletic Trainers' Association

- ◆ Founded 1950
- ◆ To "enhance the quality of health care for athletes, and those engaged in physical activity, and to advance the profession of athletic training through education and research in the prevention, evaluation, management, and rehabilitation of injuries."
- ◆ Established standards for athletic trainers through it education and certification programs.
- ◆ Publications:
  - ⊿ *Journal of Athletic Training, NATA News*

Subdiscipline Organizations

◆ North American Society for the Psychology of Sport and Physical Activity (NASPSPA)
◆ The International Association for the Philosophy of Sport (IAPS)
◆ North American Society for Sport History (NASSH)
◆ North American Society for the Sociology of Sport (NASSS)
◆ North American Society for Sport Management (NASSM)

Sport Organizations for Coaches and Professionals

◆ Examples for swim coaches:
  ↗ American Swimming Coaches Association
  ↗ Aquatics Exercise Association
  ↗ United States Masters Swimming
  ↗ United States Diving
  ↗ National Interscholastic Swimming Coaches

◆ Examples for professionals interested in tennis:
  ↗ Intercollegiate Tennis Coaches Association
  ↗ Sports On Wheels
  ↗ United States Professional Tennis Association
  ↗ United States Tennis Association
  ↗ Women's Tennis Association

Chapter 11: Teaching and Coaching Careers in Physical Education and Sport

◆ What are the advantages and disadvantages of pursuing a teaching career?

◆ What are the similarities and differences between teaching and coaching?

◆ What is the effect of burnout on teachers and coaches?

Teaching Careers

◆ School and non-school settings
  ↗ Have high expectations for all students.
  ↗ Keep students involved in relevant activities.
  ↗ Create and atmosphere that promotes learning.

◆ What are some of the reasons that people go into the teaching profession?

◆ What are *your* reasons for entering the teaching profession?

Benefits and Drawbacks of Teaching

◆ BENEFITS:
  ↗ Salary
  ↗ Teach diverse activities
  ↗ Offers job tenure
  ↗ Intrinsic rewards
  ↗ Opportunity to coach

◆ In non-school settings:
  ↗ Clients are voluntary
  ↗ Opportunity to specialize in an area

◆ DISADVANTAGES:
  ↗ Lack of financial support
  ↗ Inadequate facilities
  ↗ Discipline problems
  ↗ Overpopulated classes
  ↗ Non-subject related duties (lunch duty, etc.)

◆ In non-school settings:
  ↗ Lack job security
  ↗ Various work hours

Qualities of Effective Teachers

- ◆ Organizational skills
- ◆ Communication skills
- ◆ Instructional skills
- ◆ Motivational skills
- ◆ Human relations skills

Competencies for Beginning Teachers - NASPE

- ◆ Content knowledge
- ◆ Growth and development
- ◆ Diverse learners
- ◆ Management and Motivation

- ◆ Communication
- ◆ Learning and Instruction
- ◆ Learner Assessment
- ◆ Reflection
- ◆ Collaboration

Developmentally Appropriate Physical Activity Experiences

With the growth of physical activity programs outside of the school setting, the following elements should be considered when creating a program that is developmentally appropriate:

- ↗ Curriculum
- ↗ Movement concepts and skills
- ↗ Cognitive development
- ↗ Affective development
- ↗ Fitness concepts
- ↗ Fitness tests
- ↗ Calisthenics
- ↗ Fitness

- ↗ Assessment
- ↗ Regular involvement
- ↗ Active participation
- ↗ Activities
- ↗ Equity
- ↗ Success rate
- ↗ Time
- ↗ Facilities
- ↗ Equipment

Teaching Responsibilities

- **Instructional Tasks** (related directly to teaching)
  - ⤴ Explaining or performing a skill, or strategy, and evaluating students' performances.
- **Managerial Tasks** (related to the administration of class)
  - ⤴ Taking attendance, dealing with discipline problems, supervising the locker room, handling equipment.
- **Institutional Tasks** (related to the setting in which teaching occurs)
  - ⤴ Hall duty, lunch room supervision, attend curriculum and department meetings, conduct parent-teacher conferences.
- May conduct research
- Community Responsibilities

Teaching Careers

- School Setting
  - ⤴ K-12 (public or private)
  - ⤴ Higher education
    - » Basic instruction
    - » Professional Preparation
  - ⤴ Adapted physical education
  - ⤴ Special-Interest Schools

- Non-school Setting
  - – Clubs
  - – Community organizations
  - – Centers for the elderly
  - – Resorts
  - – Military

Teaching Certification

- Each state has minimum requirements that prospective teachers must reach before they become legally certified to teach.
- Complete standardized tests, such as PRAXIS that test:
  - ⤴ general knowledge
  - ⤴ communication skills
  - ⤴ professional knowledge
  - ⤴ specialty area (physical education or health, etc.)
- Public schools require certification, but private and non-school settings may not.

Coaching Careers

- **Why do people choose coaching careers?**
  - ↗ Love of the sport, influence on others, benefits of participating in physical activity, love of children, etc.
- **Coaching responsibilities**
  - ↗ Instructional: conducting practice, coaching a game
  - ↗ Managerial: recording statistics, dealing with equipment, giving interviews, recruiting opportunities
  - ↗ Institutional: teaching or department duties/meetings
  - ↗ Represent organization
  - ↗ Counseling athletes
  - ↗ Professional development at clinics/conventions

Benefits and Drawbacks of Coaching

- **BENEFITS:**
  - ↗ Intrinsic rewards
  - ↗ Excitement of winning
  - ↗ Respect
  - ↗ Satisfaction of giving one's best
  - ↗ Help athletes learn
- **DRAWBACKS:**
  - ↗ Long hours
  - ↗ Salaries vary greatly
  - ↗ High turnover rate
  - ↗ Pressure to win
  - ↗ Burnout

Securing a Coaching Position

- Requires a great deal of expertise gained through:
  - ↗ Playing experience
  - ↗ Attending clinics and workshops
  - ↗ Become and official in your sport
  - ↗ Take advantage of certification/licensing programs
- May require teaching certificate or master's degree depending on where and what you coach.
- May want to develop expertise in a second sport out of season to increase marketability.
- Gain practical experience however possible.

NASPE Standards for Athletic Coaches

A **framework** for the education of coaches included 8 domains:
- ↗ Injuries: Prevention, Care, and Management
- ↗ Risk Management
- ↗ Growth, Development, and Learning
- ↗ Training, Conditioning, and Nutrition
- ↗ Social/Psychological Aspects of Coaching
- ↗ Skills, Tactics, and Strategies
- ↗ Teaching and Coaching
- ↗ Professional Preparation and Development

NATIONAL ASSOCIATION FOR SPORT & PHYSICAL EDUCATION

The Coaches Code of Conduct (2001)

- ◆ Ensure that the health, well-being and development of athletes is considered over the win/loss record.
- ◆ Serve as role models.
- ◆ Exemplify honesty, integrity, fair play, and sportsmanship despite the outcomes of competition.
- ◆ Maintain professional demeanor in all relationships. Treat everyone with respect and dignity.
- ◆ Committed to the education of athletes and encourage academic achievement.

NATIONAL ASSOCIATION FOR SPORT & PHYSICAL EDUCATION

Coaching Certification Programs

- ◆ American Sport Education Program (ASEP)
  - ↗ Training in coaching the young athlete, coaching principles, sports first aid, drugs and sport, and teaching sport skills.
- ◆ National Youth Sport Coaches Association (NYSCA)
- ◆ Program for Athletic Coaches Education (PACE)

Burnout

- ◆ Overwhelming exhaustion, feelings of cynicism and detachment from the job, and a sense of ineffectiveness and lack of accomplishment.
- ◆ <u>Causes:</u>
  - ↗ Lack of administrative and community support
  - ↗ Lack of input
  - ↗ Inadequate salaries for large teaching loads
  - ↗ Large classes, discipline problems
  - ↗ Absence of opportunities for professional and personal growth
  - ↗ Teacher-coach role conflict
  - ↗ Professional and personal problem interaction

Burnout

- ◆ Prevention and remediation
  - ↗ Provide meaningful in-service programs
  - ↗ Increased feedback about performance by administration
  - ↗ Participation in professional organizations
  - ↗ Revitalize oneself on time off with hobbies or nonwork related activities
  - ↗ Maintain good health

Increasing Professional Marketability

- ☑ **Build on skills and talents**
  - ↗ Need for bilingual educators.
- ☑ **Additional coursework**
  - ↗ Adapted physical education
- ☑ **Dual certification**
  - ↗ Become certified to teach more than one subject or even driver education.
- ☑ **Practical experience**
  - ↗ Join professional organizations and network.
- ☑ **Demonstrate use of technology**

Chapter 12: Fitness- and Health-related Careers in Physical Education and Sport

◆ What are the responsibilities of a fitness or exercise specialist?

◆ What are the opportunities available for someone pursuing a therapy-related career?

◆ How does one increase their marketability for fitness-, health-, and therapy-related careers?

Fitness- and Exercise-related Careers

◆ **Preventive programs**
  - Specialists work with healthy adults to increase their level of fitness.
  - Corporate fitness centers, commercial fitness centers, and community agencies (YMCA/YWCA)

◆ **Rehabilitative programs**
  - Specialists work with individuals who exhibit the effects of coronary heart disease focusing on attaining a functional state of living and an enhanced quality of life.
  - Most often found in hospitals, medical clinics or community agencies affiliated with corporate fitness centers.

Comprehensive Wellness Program Components

◆ Fitness development and maintenance

◆ Educational efforts

◆ Health promotion

◆ Lifestyle modification

◆ Recreational sport opportunities

Program Aspects
(Institute of Aerobics Research)

◆ Medical screening

◆ Fitness and lifestyle assessment

◆ Goal setting

◆ Supervised group programs

◆ Educational classes

◆ Motivation and reinforcement

 Why should these aspects be included?

How could you implement each of these aspects?

Exercise Program Specialist Responsibilities

◆ Direct program

◆ Train and supervise staff

◆ Budget responsibilities

◆ Facility management

◆ Marketing

◆ Evaluation

◆ Individual exercise prescriptions

◆ Evaluate and counsel on lifestyle

◆ Data collection and analysis

Worksite Health Programs

◆ 46% of all worksites offer programs
  ↗ 38% of small corporations
  ↗ 68% of large corporations

◆ Potential to reach over 110 million adults
  ↗ Convenient for employees
  ↗ Offers peer and social support

◆ Economic benefits to corporations
  ↗ Reduced injury rates, lower workman's compensation costs, and reduced health care costs
  ↗ Enhancement of workplace morale, retaining employees

Top 10 Worksite Health Promotion Activities

- ◆ Job hazard/injury prevention
- ◆ Exercise/physical fitness
- ◆ Smoking control
- ◆ Stress management
- ◆ Alcohol/other drugs
- ◆ Back care
- ◆ Nutrition
- ◆ High blood pressure
- ◆ AIDS education
- ◆ Cholesterol screening

WELCOA Program Suggestions

- ◆ Voluntary participation
- ◆ Continuous marketing
- ◆ Sensitivity to individual differences
- ◆ Frequent evaluation
- ◆ Modeling of healthy behavior by staff
- ◆ Recognition and reward
- ◆ Record-keeping
- ◆ Balance between fun and clinically significant programs
- ◆ Personalize the program

Commercial and Community Fitness Programs

IHRSA

- ◆ IHRSCA
  - ↗ Club membership has increased by 51% from 1987 to 1996.
  - ↗ In 2000, there were nearly 33 million club members.
- ◆ Growth of community programs
  - ↗ **Programs for all ages**
    - » Toddlers and preschool programs have increased.
  - ↗ **Programs for all abilities**
    - » For example, The Fitness Clinic for Physically Disabled at San Diego State University
  - ↗ The addition of wellness centers have allowed hospitals to take more preventative approach!

Personal Trainers

- ◆ **Work in private and public settings**:
  - ↗ Conducting fitness assessments.
  - ↗ Developing specific goals with clients.
  - ↗ Designing programs for goal attainment.
  - ↗ Coaching clients through workouts.
  - ↗ Monitoring progress of goals.
- ◆ **New use of the Internet, email, and phone to hire personal trainers and report results for convenience.**

Strength and Conditioning Professionals

- ◆ "Assess, motivate, educate, and train athletes for the primary goal of improving sport performance." (NSCA)
- ◆ Competencies necessary in the areas of:
  - ↗ Scientific foundations of sport/exercise and nutrition
  - ↗ Exercise leadership and program design
  - ↗ Techniques of sport psychology to maximize performance
  - ↗ Risks of performance-enhancing substances

Rehabilitation Programs

- ◆ Clinical exercise physiologists work mainly in hospitals and clinics.
- ◆ Work closely with physicians to meet the needs of diverse clients.
- ◆ To plan rehabilitation programs, they must be familiar with:
  - ↗ Medical aspects of clients disease or condition
  - ↗ Limitations faced by clients
  - ↗ Drugs commonly used to treat the disease/condition and their effects
  - ↗ Psychological aspects of exercise on the clients

Career Preparation

- ◆ Education
  - ↗ Undergraduate and graduate education in exercise science, fitness and cardiac rehabilitation, etc.
- ◆ Various certifications offered by:
  - ↗ ACSM
  - ↗ YMCA
  - ↗ AFAA
  - ↗ NSCA

- ◆ Practical experience
- ◆ Professional involvement

Athletic Training National Athletic Trainers' Association

- ◆ Prevention of Injuries
  - ↗ Supervision of conditioning programs
  - ↗ Advising coaches and athletes
  - ↗ Assist with preseason physicals
  - ↗ Checking equipment and facilities for safety
- ◆ Rehabilitation
  - ↗ Administers therapeutic treatments and monitors progress.
  - ↗ Motivate and encourage throughout recovery
  - ↗ Record-keeping of injury status and history of injury
- ◆ Certification - NATA

Health and Weight-Control Clubs & Spas

- ◆ Found at resorts, hotels, mineral springs, and cruise ships.
- ◆ Are they only seeking your money?
- ◆ Offer fitness activities, graded exercise tests, instruction in sport activities, exercise classes
- ◆ Diet and nutritional counseling, stress management, massages
- ◆ Growth of commercial diet centers focused on weight reduction.

Therapy-Related Careers

- **Dance therapy (ADTA)**
  - ↗ Clients have freedom of movement and gains a sense of identity.
  - ↗ Encourages individuals to recognize and express their emotions.
  - ↗ Used with all segments of the population.
- **Recreational therapy (AAHPERD)**
  - ↗ Concerned with problems of physically, emotionally, and socially disabled persons and with the elderly.
  - ↗ Using the techniques of play, it helps achieve appropriate goals for those in community and institutional settings.
- **Kinesiotherapy (AKA)**
  - ↗ "…under the direction of a physician, treats the effects of disease, injury, and congenital disorders, through the use of therapeutic exercise and eduucation."

☑ Increasing Professional Marketability

- ◆ Additional courses in health and related areas
- ◆ Certification
  - ↗ ACSM, First Aid/CPR, NATA
- ◆ Build on one's interests and strengths
  - ↗ Develop areas of expertise that interest you.
- ◆ Practical experience
  - ↗ Internships, fieldwork, and volunteering
  - ↗ Gain diverse experiences in settings and clients.

Chapter 13: Sport Careers in Management, Media, Performance, and Related Areas

◆ What are the professional opportunities for those in sport management?

◆ How can preparation in physical education, exercise science, and sport assist individuals in sport media?

◆ How can professionals increase their marketability in these areas?

The Sport Enterprise

◆ In 2001, $ 3.5 billion was spent on fitness equipment, both home and institutional.

◆ In 2001, sales of athletic footwear topped $15.4 billion; running shoes being most popular.

◆ In 2001, $11.45 billion done in sales of sports licensed products.

◆ Sports and fitness are BIG business!

Sport Spectator Interest

◆ Attendance at sports events is rising and approaching all-time highs.

◆ Men's and women's NCAA Final Four basketball tournaments were sold out.

◆ More than 20 million fans attended regular season NBA games.

◆ The media---television, newspapers, magazines, books, and movies---have come to play an enormous role in the world of sports.

Sports and the Media

◆ Networks paid $17.6 billion to the NFL for broadcast rights through 2005.

◆ NBC paid $2.6 billion for broadcast rights for the Olympic Games through 2008.

◆ CBS paid $6 billion to telecast the NCAA men's basketball tournament for 11 years.

Sports and Salaries

◆ Average Salaries
- ⊅ NFL = $1.2 million
- ⊅ NBA = $4.2 million
- ⊅ MLB = $ 2.3 million
- ⊅ NHL = $1.5 million
- ⊅ WNBA= $55,000

◆ Tiger Woods has a $100 million contract over 5 years with Nike.

Sport Management Competencies

◆ Undergraduate education in sport management address the following areas:
- ⊅ **Behavioral dimensions in sport**
- ⊅ **Management and organization skills in sport**
- ⊅ **Ethics**
- ⊅ **Marketing in sport**
- ⊅ **Communication in sport**
- ⊅ **Economics in sport**
- ⊅ **Legal aspects of sport**
- ⊅ **Sport governance**
- ⊅ **Practicum/fieldwork and internship**

Careers in Sport Management

◆ Athletic Administration
  ↗ Director of Athletics
    » High school and Collegiate levels
    » Hiring of staff
    » Supervision of coaches, officials, and teams
    » Development and management of budget
  ↗ Specialization in athletic fundraising or compliance
◆ Director of Intramurals and/or Campus Recreation
  ↗ Promote participation in a variety of ways and means.
  ↗ National Intramural-Recreational Sports Association

Careers in Sport Management

◆ Director of Corporate Recreation
  ↗ Provide recreational and sport opportunities for those in the corporate setting.
  ↗ Set up teams, schedule contests, provide instruction, and supervise.
◆ Sport Facilities Management
  ↗ Found in almost any setting; the primary concern is the safety of the individuals using the facility through knowledge of building codes, health and sanitation requirements, and certain laws.
  ↗ Scheduling of events, ticket sales, concessions, or parking.
◆ Sport Retailing
  ↗ The sale of sporting goods
  ↗ Creation of new markets with the increase of active women.
  ↗ Salespersons and manufacturers' representatives

Career Opportunities in Professional Organizations

◆ AAPHERD, NCAA, NFSHSA, LPGA, USTA, NHL, etc…
◆ Athletic conferences (Commissioner of Big Ten, etc…)
◆ Foundations such as the Women's Sport Foundation
◆ Entry level jobs deal with day-to-day operations.
◆ Fundraising, public relations, conducting membership drives, writing and editing publications, and analyzing statistical data.

Careers in Sport Media

- ◆ Sport Broadcasting
  - ↗ Requires knowledge of the game: skills, strategies, rules, officiating
  - ↗ Ability to communicate clearly.
  - ↗ National Sportscasters and Sportswriters Association (NSSA)
- ◆ Sportswriting and Journalism
  - ↗ May cover events live or write feature articles.
  - ↗ Research stories, compile statistics, interview athletes and coaches
  - ↗ Ability to meet deadlines while traveling and working long hours.
- ◆ Sport Photography
  - ↗ Newspapers, sport publications, and freelance work
  - ↗ Maintain portfolio of work, gain practical experience

Careers in Sport Media

- ◆ Sports Information Director
  - ↗ Promote athletic events through various forms of media.
  - ↗ Maintain records, compile statistics, prepare promotional brochures, game-day programs, maintain web pages.
  - ↗ Writes press releases, and arranges press conferences/interviews
  - ↗ College Sports Information Directors of America (COSIDA)
- ◆ Web Developer
  - ↗ Design, create, and update sites for college athletic departments, professional teams, sports organizations, newspapers, and television networks.

Performance and Other Sport Careers

- ◆ **Dance Careers**
  - ↗ Professional dancer, dance teacher, dance therapist, or dance administration in dance companies
- ◆ **Professional Athletics**
  - ↗ Only 1.3% of NCAA men's basketball players go pro; football---2%, baseball---10.5%, although opportunities are growing.
- ◆ **Officiating**
  - ↗ Part-time or full-time careers
  - ↗ Certification required at most levels---must know rules of sport as well as good officiating mechanics.
- ◆ **Sport Law**
  - ↗ Requires completion of law school
  - ↗ Teach classes in sport law and management or become agents for professional athletes: negotiate contracts and financial consultants

Entrepreneurship

- ◆ Should I be an entrepreneur? Ask yourself two questions first:
  - ↗ Do I have a viable, marketable service or product?
  - ↗ Is there a consumer desire for the service or product?
- ◆ **Examples:**
  - ↗ Personal trainers
  - ↗ Consultants
  - ↗ Mobile fitness and health appraisal business
  - ↗ Personal coaching
  - ↗ Computerized skill analysis
  - ↗ Sport instructional camps and schools

Increasing Your Professional Marketability

- ◆ Education
- ◆ Development of talent
- ◆ Build on experiences progressively
  - ↗ Entry level positions
  - ↗ Career ladder
- ◆ Fieldwork and Internships
- ◆ Volunteer work
- ◆ Networking

Chapter 14: Issues and Challenges in Physical Education and Sport

◆ How are the roles of physical education, exercise science, and sport professionals in the consumer education movement relative to physical activity?

◆ What are some strategies that professionals could use to promote daily physical education throughout the country?

◆ What are some strategies that could be used to promote lifespan involvement in physical activity and sport?

Issues in Physical Education and Sport

- ◆ Gambling
- ◆ Drug Abuse
- ◆ Increasing Salaries
- ◆ Violence
- ◆ Burnout of young athletes
- ◆ Professionalization of collegiate athletics
- ◆ Racism

- ◆ Academic qualifications of athletes
- ◆ Emphasis on winning in youth sports
- ◆ Accountability of teachers
- ◆ Integrity of PE as a school subject
- ◆ Equity

Issues in Physical Education and Sport

- ◆ Leadership in physical activity movement
- ◆ Promotion of affective development
- ◆ Leadership of youth sport programs
- ◆ Growing field of physical education and sport
- ◆ Closing the gap between research and practice

Challenges in Physical Education and Sport

- ◆ Daily quality physical education K-12
- ◆ Advocacy
- ◆ Attainment of national health objectives
- ◆ Lifelong involvement in physical activity for all people

Leadership in Physical Activity Movement

- ◆ **We have a responsibility to educate the public about the benefits of physical activity and fitness.**
  - ↗ National Coalition for Promoting Physical Activity (NCPPA)
- ◆ **Consumer education about which programs meet health standards.**
- ◆ **Professionals' leadership in physical activity and fitness movement**
  - ↗ Corbin: Seek active leadership roles
  - ↗ Ewers: Be "pace setters" of the exercise parade
  - ↗ "Because it falls within our domain."

Teaching Values in Physical Education and Sport

- ◆ Development of values, character, and ethical decision-making skills has long been touted as one of our primary purposes.
- ◆ Values developed include:

  - ↗ **Cooperation**
  - ↗ **Self-discipline**
  - ↗ **Fair play**
  - ↗ **Emotional control**
  - ↗ **Teamwork**
  - ↗ **Self-esteem and self-confidence**

Teaching Values in Physical Education and Sport

- ◆ Ethical and moral abuses associated with sport at all levels has received increased attention.
- ◆ Use of physical education practices that humiliate, embarrass, and belittle students have been tolerated.
  - ↗ How do these practices enhance individual development?
  - ↗ How do these practices contribute to lifespan involvement?
- ◆ Careful planning by professionals is needed in order to structure programs to promote the development of values and ethics.

Teaching Values in Physical Education and Sport

- ◆ Promoting an active lifestyle can be enhanced by the development of affective behavior in our program participants:
  - ↗ **Confidence in their abilities as movers**
  - ↗ **Sense of self-worth**
  - ↗ **Appreciation of the value of health and the contribution of physical activity to well-being**
- ◆ Provide more individualized programs if it will empower participants to take responsibility for their lives.

Leadership in Youth Sport

- ◆ Youth sports programs involve over 25 million boys and girls and 3 million adult volunteers.
- ◆ Purpose of youth sports:
  - ↗ **Promote the healthy physical, psychological, and social development of participants.**
- ◆ Criticism of youth sports
  - ↗ **Overemphasis on winning and competition.**
  - ↗ **Losing sight of the developmental focus of youth sports.**
- ◆ Need for physical education and sport professionals to assume a greater role in the conduct of youth sports.

Young Athletes' Bill of Rights

◆ Offers parents and coaches guidance in structuring a sport experience...
  ↗ **Opportunity to participate regardless of ability.**
  ↗ **Participation at a level that is commensurate with each child's developmental level.**
  ↗ **Qualified adult leadership.**
  ↗ **Shared leadership and decision-making.**
  ↗ **Right to play as a child and not as an adult.**
  ↗ **Proper preparation.**
  ↗ **Equal opportunity to strive for success.**
  ↗ **Treatment with dignity.**
  ↗ **Have fun through sport.**

Leadership in Youth Sport (Seefeldt)

◆ "Youth sports programs are neither inherently good nor bad."... Their value depends on the quality of adult leadership and the supporting environment."
◆ Volunteers should focus on promoting continued sport involvement of children rather than on winning.
◆ Volunteers should be aware of the reason's children participate in youth sport and try to incorporate them into every practice:
  ↗ **Fun**
  ↗ **Learn skills**
  ↗ **Be with their friends**
  ↗ **Excitement of competition on their own terms**

Improving Youth Sports (Seefeldt)

◆ Make changes to accommodate children of all abilities and interests.
◆ Continue research in order to base programs on sound principles.
◆ Develop and implement sound training programs for coaches.

Leadership in Youth Sports (Martens)

◆ Provide experiences that will "turn kids on to physical activity for the lifetime."
  ↗ Positive, Fun
  ↗ Increase self-worth
◆ Principle's for Youth Sport:
  ↗ Modeling principle
  ↗ Reinforcement principle
  ↗ Self-determination principle
  ↗ Self-worth principle
  ↗ Fun principle

The Growing Field of Physical Education and Sport

◆ Since the late 1960s, there has been an **increased depth and breadth** of the field.
◆ Development of the **subdisicplines** has lead to research traditions, professional organizations, and publications new and expanded career opportunities.
  ↗ However, the numerous subdisciplines have raised concerns about fragmentation and specialization of the field.
◆ Important to recognize the role of each of the subdisciplines in achieving our mission of helping people to be physically active throughout their lifespan.

The Field of Physical Education and Sport

◆ There still remains the need to integrate our knowledge to better respond to the needs of individuals with whom we work.
◆ Is it time for a "new" name for the field?
  ↗ Do we have a "confused identity that lacks an accurate concept of who we are, what we do, and where we are going?"
◆ Professional commitment to further growth of the field through teacher preparation and professional organizations.

The Gap Between Research and Practice

- Time lag between publication of research and the utilization of relevant findings.
- Critical to narrow the gap so that our programs are based on sound current principles.
- A diversity of factors contribute to this gap:
  - Practitioner factors
    - Inadequate knowledge of research methods, lack of communication between researchers and practitioners, negative attitude towards research, lack of time and resources
  - Researcher factors
    - Conflicting results of studies due to poorly designed studies, researcher's lack of concern for application of findings

Closing the Gap Between Research and Practice

- Professional preparation programs better preparing students to interpret research and utilize the findings.
- Practitioners and researchers working collaboratively to investigate problems.
- Researchers addressing practical applications of their work when reporting findings.
- Research **"translators"**:
  - Consolidate findings, identify practical applications, and disseminate easy-to-understand information through newsletters and journals.

High-Quality Daily Physical Education

- Regular, appropriate physical activity can contribute to good health and enhance the quality of life for people of all ages.
- Therefore physical activity should start at an early age.
  - Daily PE can reach 51 million children and youth and help them learn the skills, knowledge, and values necessary to incorporate physical activity into their lifestyles.
  - Daily PE has been encouraged for all students K-12 since 1987, with the National Physical Education Resolution or House Concurrent Resolution 97.

Components of a Quality Program (NASPE)

◆ Provides evidence of its effectiveness through assessment of outcomes.
◆ Provides daily opportunities for the development of skills and fitness.
◆ Fosters an understanding of why, when, and how physical activity can be incorporated into one's lifestyle.

NATIONAL ASSOCIATION
FOR SPORT & PHYSICAL
EDUCATION

Components of a Quality Program (NASPE)

◆ Focuses on acquisition and maintenance of health-related benefits of physical activity.
◆ Promotes the development of skills for participation beyond the school years.
◆ Accommodates the needs and developmental levels of all students.
◆ Teachers students how to apply the concepts of exercise in their daily lives.

NATIONAL ASSOCIATION
FOR SPORT & PHYSICAL
EDUCATION

High-quality Daily Physical Education

◆ PE should be taught by **certified** physically educators.

◆ Each teacher must support the crusade for high-quality daily PE.

◆ Importance of shaping healthy behaviors, during the early years; harder to change unhealthy habits.

◆ Capitalize on current societal interest in wellness, fitness, and physical activity. Don't Wait!!!

Advocacy

- ◆ Physical education and sport professionals must take an active role in promoting their programs.
  - ↗ **Use of effective communication to influence others.**
- ◆ Must capitalize on societal interest in sport, physical fitness, and health otherwise there will be continued:
  - ↗ decline of PE programs in schools
  - ↗ increased privatization of sports
  - ↗ need for for health promotion and physical activity programs in the worksite, community, and medical settings.
- ◆ Important to market programs to gain support and to involve more people.

 ## Advocacy

- ◆ Our responsibility to address the tremendous disparities that still exist in physical activity and disease conditions according to race, ethnicity, age, sex, education, sexual orientation, ability/disability, and income.
- ◆ Increase access to, and promotion of quality programs.
- ◆ NASPE:
  - ↗ May is National Physical Fitness and Sports Month
  - ↗ May 1 to May 7: National Physical Education and Sport Week
- ◆ AAHPERD and American Heart Association
  - ↗ Jump Rope for Heart
  - ↗ Hoops for Heart

Advocacy

- ◆ National Girls and Women in Sports Day
  - ↗ Promotes the increase of opportunities in sport for girls and women.
- ◆ Passage of state and federal legislation
  - ↗ Physical Education for Progress Act (PEP)
- ◆ Use various forms of media to reach people.
- ◆ Contact organizations that promote physical activity and health and ask them to become more "proactive."

Goals of Healthy People 2010

◆ To help individuals of all ages increase life expectancy and improve their quality of life.

◆ To eliminate health disparities among segments of the population, including differences that occur by gender, race or ethnicity, education or income, disability, geographic location, or sexual orientation.

Achievement of National Health Objectives

◆ Take an active role in working with other health professionals.

◆ Personal commitment of physical education and sport professionals to be role models for healthy, active lifestyles.

◆ Attaining these goals with lead to an increased public recognition of the worth and value of our field, as well as increased employment opportunities.

Lifespan Involvement for All People

◆ Expansion of physical education,sport programs, and services to new settings and population groups.
- ↗ Preschoolers
- ↗ Adults
- ↗ Elderly
- ↗ Persons with disabilities

◆ Increased recognition that regular and appropriate physical activity can make a vital contribution to the health throughout the lives of all people.

Lifespan Involvement for All People

- ◆ Enhancement of quality of life and longevity.
- ◆ For maximum benefits, healthy habits should be developed early in life.
- ◆ Growth of sport involvement for all ages and abilities.
- ◆ Changes in our programs to accommodate a wider range of individual differences.
  - ↗ Culturally competent and developmentally appropriate physical education programs.

Lifespan Involvement for All People

- ◆ Access to programs for underserved populations is critical.
  - ↗ Growth of commercial programs for those who can afford to pay will limit participation by those who can not afford the fees.
  - ↗ Access should be available to all individuals regardless of socioeconomic background.
- ◆ Professional preparation for students to work with an increasingly diverse population across the lifespan.

Chapter 15: Future of Physical Education and Sport

◆ How can physical education, exercise science, and sport professionals capitalize on the public's interest in health and physical activity?

◆ How will technological advances influence physical education, exercise science, and sport?

◆ What can the field of physical education, exercise science, and sport do to improve its delivery system?

Future

◆ What is our vision for physical education and sport in the 21st century?

◆ Physical education and sport professionals must take an active role in charting our future goals and working toward their attainment.

Future

◆ Achieving the future of our choice requires:

☑ Strong leadership

☑ A charted course designed to achieve our goals

☑ Marshaled efforts and resources

☑ Active involvement of professionals at all levels in pursuit of theses goals.

Futurists

- ◆ Describe the future.
- ◆ Predict the course of past and current events.
- ◆ Identify consequences of selected courses of action.
- ◆ Define priorities that will lead to the future of choice.
- ◆ Use techniques such as:
  - ⬈ Expert advice
  - ⬈ Trend extrapolation
  - ⬈ Technological forecasting
  - ⬈ Scenarios

Future Effects of Trends

- ◆ If the direction of the trend continues, what will be some positive and/or negative consequences?
- ◆ If the rate or the speed of the trend continues, what will be some positive and/or negative consequences?
- ◆ What will occur if the trend levels off or reverses itself?
- ◆ What forces are acting to perpetuate this trend? Will these forces continue in the future?
- ◆ How much of this trend is "shapeable" by human action?
- ◆ What type of action would it take to modify the trend?

Health Promotion and Disease Prevention

- ◆ Wellness Movement
  - ⬈ Individual responsibility for health.
  - ⬈ Integration of several components, including nutrition, physical activity, stress management, and elimination of risk factors.
  - ⬈ Increased interest by the corporate sector in wellness.
- ◆ National health reports
  - ⬈ Healthy People
  - ⬈ Objectives for the Nation
  - ⬈ Healthy People 2000
  - ⬈ Healthy People 2010

Health Promotion and Disease Prevention

◆ Physical Activity and Fitness Movement
  ↗ Increased evidence supporting the contribution of physical activity to health.
  ↗ Must reach children, youths, and adults leading sedentary lives and involve them in our programs.
  ↗ Leadership in physical activity and fitness.
  ↗ Further expansion of programs to nonschool settings.

Health Promotion and Disease Prevention

◆ Health Care Reform
  ↗ In 2000, health care costs exceeded $1.3 trillion dollars and accounted for over 13.2% of the Gross Domestic Product.
  ↗ Increase emphasis on early intervention, health promotion programs, and disease prevention because these efforts can lead to the reduction of health care costs.
  ↗ Implement social and behavioral interventions.
  ↗ A national health care plan has still not been approved.

Education

◆ Education should be looked as a lifelong experience and schools should be the resource for it.
◆ The structure of school is changing with the increase in technology and the flexibility it offers.
◆ The school as a community learning center, offering programs before and after school, weekends, and summers.

Education and Physical Education

To retain physical education as an integral part of society, physical educators must:

- ↗ Strengthen physical education as a significant part of the educational curriculum.
- ↗ Expand instructional programs to adult learners.
- ↗ Prepare students to be lifelong learners.
- ↗ Play an active role in school community learning centers.

Technology:
"Making the future different from the past."

- ◆ **Unprecedented efforts on research in our field.**
- ◆ **Use computers to perform a myriad of tasks.**
  - ↗ Record-keeping
  - ↗ Fitness profiling
  - ↗ Database management
- ◆ **Contribution to improved performance.**
  - ↗ Enhanced skill technique in many sports.
  - ↗ Development of advanced equipment and apparel.
- ◆ **Biotechnology**
  - ↗ Tissue engineering, muscle fiber typing, cloning

WEB Technology

- ◆ Equipment:
  - ↗ Computerized muscle ergometers
  - ↗ Electronic gas analyzers
- ◆ Internet
- ◆ Internet telephones
- ◆ World Wide Web
- ◆ E-mail
- ◆ Microcomputers
- ◆ Videoconferencing
- ◆ Multimedia instruction
- ◆ Distance learning
- ◆ Virtual reality

Changing Demographics

- **Shift in the age distribution of the population due to:**
  - ↗ Increasing life expectancy
  - ↗ Declining birthrate
- **Growth of population 65 years and over**
  - ↗ 1900 ... 4%
  - ↗ 1997 ... 12.7%
  - ↗ 2015 ... 18.5% estimated
- **Growth of population 85 years and older**
  - ↗ From 3.8 million in 1996 to over 7 million in 2025.
- **Increase in minorities 65 years and older**
  - ↗ Projected growth from 13% in 1996 to 25% in 2030.

Cultural Diversity

- Increase in minority population in U.S.
  - ↗ By 2035, estimated that 40% of population will be comprised of minorities.
- They face many barriers to accessing health care, including low socioeconomic status and the language barrier, thus increasing their risk for disease.
- What will be the impact of minority health on the nation?

Changing Structure of the Family

- Increase in number of single parent families.
- Increase in dual career families.
- "Latch-key" children come home after school to little if any adult supervision.
- Increase in preschool and day care programs.
- Growing threats to the health and well-being of children and youth.
  - » Drug and alcohol abuse
  - » Violence
  - » Child abuse
  - » Suicide
  - » Risky sexual behaviors

Changing Populations and Physical Education and Sport

- **Prepare to work with aging and increasing diverse population groups.**
- **Develop culturally competent techniques of teaching.**
- **Provide physical education and sport opportunities for economically disadvantaged.**
- **Growth of interrelationships between schools, families, and health.**
  - ↗ What is the role of physical education, exercise science, and sport professionals in these relationships?

Integrated Approach for the Well-Being of Children

- ◆ Coordinated School Health Model developed by the CDC.
- ◆ The following 8 components in schools that have an impact on the well-being of children:
  - ↗ Health education
  - ↗ Physical education
  - ↗ Health services
  - ↗ Nutrition services
  - ↗ Health promotion for staff
  - ↗ Counseling and psychological services
  - ↗ Healthy school environment
  - ↗ Parent/community involvement

CDC SAFER • HEALTHIER • PEOPLE™

Expanding Frontiers

- ◆ The question is not, "*WILL* we ever live in space or underwater, but *WHEN* will these things become a reality?"
- ◆ Physical education and sport professionals must be prepared to help people live in their ever-changing environments.
  - ↗ Conduct research
  - ↗ Design appropriate exercise programs

Enhancing Physical Education and Sport's Quality and Effectiveness (Oberle)

- ◆ Establish minimum standards of competency.
- ◆ Develop programs and services that are flexible to meet changing needs.
- ◆ Develop meaningful programs to meet today's and tomorrow's needs.
- ◆ Reduce ineffective programs.
- ◆ Establish minimum standards for entry into professional preparation programs.

Enhancing Physical Education and Sport's Quality and Effectiveness (Oberle)

- ◆ Provide high-quality experiences for professionals within the discipline.
- ◆ Develop a system for relicensure for all professionals.
- ◆ Establish professional accrediting agencies.
- ◆ Develop high-quality model programs and build facilities that can serve as a model for the profession.

Establishment of Jurisdiction over Our Domain

- ◆ Two credentials are necessary to become publicly recognized leaders:
- ◆ Credential 1
  - ↗ A systematic knowledge base that describes the unique social service rendered by our professionals.
    - » Support the art and science of human movement.
    - » Document that our field fosters human growth and development.
    - » Show benefits from developing the proper relationship between the body, mind, and spirit.

Establishment of Jurisdiction over Our Domain

◆ <u>Credential 2</u>
  ↗ Program priorities that provide consumers with self-direction.
    » <u>Knowledge</u>
      ◆ Science of human movement and the health benefits of appropriate physical activity.
      ◆ Improved communication of scientific findings to professionals.
    » <u>Skills</u>
      ◆ Teaching of skills becomes increasingly scientific.
      ◆ Incorporation of technology to increase effectiveness of performance.

Establishment of Jurisdiction over Our Domain

◆ <u>Credential 3</u>
  ↗ Physical education teaching will continue to grow as a science and an art.
    » Improved learning outcomes
    » Accountability

Establishment of Jurisdiction over Our Domain

◆ As professionals, we must assume leadership in many areas of our field.
  ↗ Develop diverse programs to meet the needs of increasingly diverse populations.
  ↗ Strengthen programs so they are of high quality.
  ↗ Accountability
  ↗ Program promotion

Enhancement of Our Delivery Systems

The following are some changes that need to be made to enhance the effectiveness of our delivery systems:

- ↗ **Greater responsiveness to individual needs**
- ↗ **Rendering of services to new frontiers of space and underwater**
- ↗ **Closer articulation between school and community programs to:**
  - » Ensure efficient use of facilities, equipment, and personnel.
  - » Eliminate overlapping.
  - » Provide for progression throughout life in the program of activities.
- ↗ **Extensive use of new learning technologies**
- ↗ **Greater use of computers**

Preparing for the Future:

- ◆ Professionals in the field must do the following:
  - ↗ Acquisition of proper credentials to establish jurisdiction over our domain.
  - ↗ Utilization of technological advances to improve our delivery system.
  - ↗ Provide for space and underwater living.
  - ↗ Become a positive role model for a fit and health lifestyle.
  - ↗ Help persons become increasing responsible for their own health and fitness.

Preparing for the Future:

- ◆ Professionals in the field must do the following:
  - ↗ Recognize that individuals will live longer and become more fit and active.
  - ↗ Provide for all persons throughout their lifespan.
  - ↗ Remember that we are involved with the development of the whole person.
  - ↗ Make a commitment to conduct high-quality programs that are sensitive to individual needs to that physical education and sport's potential to enhance the health and quality of life for all people can be fulfilled.

Preparing for the Future

- ◆ "...at no time in the history of AAHPERD have we ...seen more opportunities for professional growth and service within the entire profession."
- ◆ The vision of lifespan involvement in physical activity for all people is a powerful one.
- ◆ Strive for excellence in all your professional endeavors.